FALUN BUDDHA LAW
(ESSENTIALS FOR FURTHER ADVANCES)

法 輪 佛 法
（精 進 要 旨）

(English Version)
（英 文 版）

LI HONGZHI

作 者 近 照

旋法至極

佛法無邊

法輪常轉

這個法輪圖形是宇宙的縮影,他在其他各個空間也有他存在的形式、演化過程,所以我說是一個世界。

— 李洪志

CONTENTS

On Buddha Law

"Buddha Law" is most profound. It is the most mystical and supernormal science of all theories in the world. To open up this field, it is necessary to make a fundamental change in the mentality of ordinary people; otherwise the truth of the cosmos will forever remain a myth to mankind and ordinary people will always crawl along within the boundary delimited by their own ignorance.

What is "Buddha Law" after all? Is it a religion? A philosophy? That is only the understanding of "the modernistic scholars of Buddhism". They merely study the theory. They regard "Buddha Law" as something like a category of philosophy and make a study of and do the so-called research on it with a critical eye. Nevertheless, "Buddha Law" is more than that little bit recorded in the Sutras, which only deals with "Buddha Law" at the elementary level. "Buddha Law" is an insight into all mysteries of the cosmos and encompasses everything while leaving out nothing from the particle, the molecule to the universe, from even the smallest to the greatest. "Buddha Law" is an exposition of the cosmic qualities "Zhen Shan Ren" (真善忍 Truth Compassion Forbearance) presented at different levels in different ways. It is what the Tao School means by "Tao" and Buddha School by "Law".

Well advanced as contemporary human science is, it is only a portion of the mysteries of the cosmos. Whenever we mention some specific phenomena concerning "Buddha Law", somebody will say: "We are now in the electronic age! Why bother with these out-of-date superstitions when science is so progressive that spaceships have even reached other planets?" As a matter of fact, no matter how advanced a computer is, it is no match for the human brain, which remains an unfathomable enigma. No matter how far our spaceships can fly, they are unable to get out of the physical world in which we human beings dwell. The knowledge of contemporary human beings or what they know is just skin-deep, and too far from the real understanding of the truth of the cosmos. Some people even dare not face up to, dare not approach or dare not admit the facts of the existing objective phenomena because these people are too conservative and unwilling to change their traditional mentality. Nothing but "Buddha Law" can thoroughly reveal the secrets of the cosmos, time and space and the human body. It can genuinely distinguish between good and evil, right and wrong, and establish the right view by eradicating all fallacies.

The guiding ideology of the present day human science can only be confined to the physical world for its development and research. It follows such a way that a subject will not be studied until it is recognized. As for the existing objective phenomena, which are invisible and intangible but reflected in our physical space in concrete forms, people dare not approach them and regard them as unidentified phenomena. Those opinionated people argue stubbornly and groundlessly that they are natural phenomena. Those with ulterior motives simply put labels of superstition on all of them against their conscience. Those who make little effort to seek truth evade them using as an excuse the under-development of the science. If human beings can change their rigid mentality and have a new understanding of themselves and the cosmos, they will make a leap forward. "Buddha

Law" can provide humankind with an insight into the immeasurable and boundless worlds for them. Throughout the ages, nothing but "Buddha Law" can give a perfect and clear exposition of humankind, all different spaces of material existence, life and the whole cosmos.

Li Hongzhi
June 2, 1992

Rich And Virtuous

The ancients said: money is something external. Everybody knows, but everybody seeks it. A strong man wants it to satisfy his desires; a woman long for it to provide her with glamour and luxury; the elderly need it to look after things he will leave behind; a wise man wants it for glory; a government official fulfils his duty for it and the like. So all seek it.

And the worse, one contends for it. An aggressive one will take risks for it; a hot-tempered one will resort to violence to gain it; a jealous one will even die for it. Enriching the people is an art for monarch and his subjects, while worshiping money is one of the worst things one can do. Being rich but without virtue harms everyone, while being rich and virtuous is what the people all hope for. For this reason, the rich ones cannot do without preaching virtue.

One accumulates virtue before one's birth. Monarch and his subjects, wealth and rank all originate from virtue. Nothing can be achieved without virtue, and loss of virtue means loss of all. Therefore, those who strive for power and seek wealth must first of all accumulate virtues. Performing good deeds as well as suffering hardships can accumulate all virtues. To do so one must understand the law of causation. By knowing this, government and its people can restrain their hearts, and the world will enjoy riches and peace.

Li Hongzhi
January 27, 1995

Broad And Profound

The theory of Falun Dafa can give guidance to anyone who cultivates, including those with religious beliefs. This Law is the Principle of the universe, the true Law that has never been revealed. In the past human beings were not allowed to know the Principle of the universe (Buddha Law); it transcends all the sciences and moral principles of ordinary human society from ancient times to the present. What has been taught in religions and what people have experienced are only superficialities and phenomena, while the Law's broad and profound inner meaning can only present itself to and be felt and understood by the practitioners who are at different levels of their true cultivation, and they can truly see what the Law is about.

Li Hongzhi
February 6,1995

True Cultivation

My disciples of true cultivation, what I teach you are the Law for cultivation of Buddha and cultivation of Tao. But you pour out your grievances to me for having suffered losses of your personal interests, rather than feel worried about the attachments you cannot let go of among ordinary people. Is this cultivation? Whether you can let go of the heart of an ordinary person is a fatal pass for you to become a real supernormal person. Every disciple of true cultivation must go through it, for this is the boundary line between a practitioner and an ordinary person.

As a matter of fact, when you feel your fame, interest and feelings harmed among ordinary people and become worried, it means that you still cling to the attachments of ordinary people. You must remember this: cultivation itself is not so painful; the crux of the matter is to let go of the attachments of ordinary people. Only when you want to let go of your fame, gain and emotions will you feel pain.

You dropped down from the holy, pure and incomparably splendid world because you had developed your attachments in that dimension. When you have fallen into the filthiest world by comparison, you do not endeavour to cultivate yourselves so that you can return as soon as possible, instead, you firmly hold on to those filthy things of the filthy world and even feel a great agony for a small loss of them. Do you know that? The Buddha once begged for food among ordinary people in order to save you, and today I have opened a great door, and teach you the Great Law to save you again. I never feel pain for the countless hardships I have endured, and what else can you not let go of? Can you bring into the paradise the things which you cannot give up in your heart along with you?

Li Hongzhi
May 22, 1995

Sagacity

When I have told some practitioners that drastic thoughts result from the karma of thoughts, and now many practitioners call all their oftentimes bad thoughts the karma of thoughts. This is not correct. Is there anything for you to cultivate if you have no bad thoughts?! Aren't you a Buddha when you are so pure? This is a wrong understanding. The karma of thoughts is when your mind vehemently reflects dirty thoughts or condemns the teacher, the Great Law, other people, etc., and you cannot get rid of such thoughts or keep them under control. However, there are also some weak ones, but they are different from general normal thoughts or ideas. You must be clear about this.

Li Hongzhi
May 23,1995

Awakening

In the world of multitudinous mortal beings, pearls and fish eyes are jumbled together. Tathagata descends to the world without being noticed. When he teaches the Law, there must be interference from evil ways. The Tao and the evil are spread at the same time and in the same world. The truth and the false are mingled, and enlightenment is most important. How to distinguish them? There must be people with good inborn qualities. As a matter of consequence, those who really have predestined relationship and can awake to it will come one after another, following the Tao and attaining the Law. They will be able to distinguish right from evil, receive the true scriptures, lighten their bodies, enrich their wisdom, fill their hearts, and take the Law boat, leisurely and carefree. Well done! Do make further advances till their consummation.

People with poor enlightenment in the corrupted world live for money, die for power, experience joy or worry over a tiny profit. They compete bitterly against each other, thus accumulating karma throughout their whole lives. When such people hear the Law, they laugh at it. Spitting out the word "superstition" from their mouths, they find it hard to understand and believe it in their hearts. Such people are regarded as having poor inborn qualities. It is hard to save them, who have so much karma that their bodies are shrouded in it, their wisdom is sealed and their true nature is lost.

Li Hongzhi
June 14, 1995

Why One Cannot See

Seeing is believing, and not seeing is not believing. That is a view of a person with poor inborn qualities. Men are lost and have accumulated much karma. How can they see when their true nature is lost? Awakening goes before seeing. Cultivate your mind and eliminate your karma, and you will be able to see when your true nature comes out. However, a person with good inborn qualities achieves the consummation by his enlightenment no matter whether he can see or not. Many others may or may not see, which is determined by their levels and inborn qualities. A practitioner usually can not see because he has a desire to see. Persisting in such an attachment, he is not able to see until he abandons it. More often than not, this results from the obstruction of one's karma or the impropriety of circumstances, or a particular way of cultivation. There is a multitude of causes varying from person to person. One is able to see but without a very clear vision, which may make it possible for him to awake to the Tao. If one is able to see everything clearly as if he were personally on the scene, then he has opened his cultivation energy and can no longer cultivate himself, because there is nothing for him to awake to.

Li Hongzhi
June 16, 1995

Learning the Law

When learning the Great Law, intellectuals should take care to avoid a most conspicuous problem, that is, they learn the Great Law in the same way as ordinary people study theoretical writings, such as selecting some relevant quotations from famous people for the examination of their actions. Such a way of learning the Great Law will hinder a practitioner in his improvement. Some other people hear that the Great Law has a very profound inner meaning and there is something very high in it for the guidance of cultivation at different levels, so they dig into every single word but find nothing in the end. These long developed habits in the study of political theory are also a factor affecting cultivation, which results in one's misinterpretation of the Law.

When you learn the Law, don't select the parts which are aimed at your problem and learn with the intention of resolving it. In fact, this is also an attachment in disguised form (not including the case in which one has a problem to be solved at once). To have a good command of the Great Law, you have no alternative but to learn it without any intention. Each time you finish reading *Zhuan Falun* and have achieved some understandings, you have made progress this way. Even if you have understood only one thing after reading it through, you have really improved as well.

As a matter of fact, you are making progress bit by bit without your realizing it in your cultivation. Keep this in mind: want nothing and you'll gain naturally.

Li Hongzhi
September 9, 1995

How to Give Assistance

Many assistants in different parts of the country have a very high understanding of the Great Law. They set a good example with their conduct and do a good organizing job in their practice sites. However, there are also some assistants who have not done so well, mainly due to their working methods. For instance, in order to make the practitioners listen to them so that it would be easy to carry out the work, some assistants use a commanding method to do the job. This is no good. The learning of the Law should be voluntary. If the learner is not willing to follow, nothing can be solved. Instead, there will arise conflicts. If it is not corrected, the conflicts will become acute and the learning of the Law will thus be badly disrupted.

What is more, in order to make practitioners believe and obey them, some assistants often use some side-street news or something sensational to raise their reputation or try to show originality. This isn't any good, either. Our assistants are voluntarily working for others, they are not the masters, so they should never have such an attachment.

How can we do the assistance work well, then? First of all, you should put yourself among the practitioners. Do not have the mind that you are above other practitioners. When there is something you do not know in your work, you should be modest and have a discussion about it with them. If you have done something wrong, you should say sincerely to the practitioners, "I am also a practitioner just as you are, so I cannot avoid making mistakes in my work. Now that I have done it wrong, let's do it according to what is right." If you have a sincere wish to let all the practitioners make joint efforts to do the work well, you will see what result you have achieved. Nobody will say you are good for nothing. Instead, they will feel that you have a good grasp of the Law, and you are open-minded and aboveboard. In fact, here is the Great Law, and every practitioner is learning it. The practitioners will measure every act and every move of the assistant, whether it is good or not, by the Great Law, and they can see it clearly. Once you have the intention of building yourself up, the practitioners will think that something has gone wrong with your Xinxing (mind-nature). Therefore, being modest you can do your work well. Your reputation comes from your good command of the Law. As a practitioner, how can you be free from faults?

Li Hongzhi
September 10, 1995

Vault

    Man shall never be able to learn the vastness of the Universe and the immensity of the Celestial Body. Man shall never be able to explore the microcosm of matter. Mankind's knowledge about the human body is merely a scratch on the surface of the profound and subtle subject. The multifarious and complex life shall remain an eternal mystery to mankind.

Li Hongzhi
September 24, 1995

Realms

A wicked person is obsessed with selfishness, spite, caused by jealousy, and complains that he is not fairly treated.

A virtuous person always keeps a heart of compassion. With no discontent, hatred, he takes hardship as joy.

An enlightened one has no attachment at all. He quietly watches the common people being lost in illusions.

Li Hongzhi
September 25, 1995

What Is Emptiness

What is Emptiness? Free from attachments is the true state of emptiness. It does not mean that there is no existence of matter. However, Zen Buddhism has come to the Period of Decline and has nothing to teach. With the Dharma disrupted in the Period of Decline, there are some learners who firmly hold on to its theory of Emptiness, flighty and crazy, as if having awakened to the essence of philosophy. Its founder Dharmer said that his doctrine could only last for six generations and after that there would be nothing to teach. Why not awake to it? If all is empty with no Law, no Buddha, no image, no self and no existence, what is Dharmer? If there is no Law, what is Zen Buddhism's theory of Emptiness? If there is no Buddha, no image, what is Sakyamuni? If there is no name, no image, no self, no existence and all is empty, why do you have to eat and drink? Why do you have to wear clothes? Would it be all right to dig your eyes out? How is it possible for you to be attached to the seven emotions and six carnal desires of an ordinary person? Actually, the Emptiness taught by the Tathagata means that one is totally free from the attachments of an ordinary person. Non-omission is the true meaning of Emptiness. The universe is originally stored with, formed from, and inhabited by matter, how can it be empty? A Law is certainly short-lived if not handed down by a Tathagata and it will disappear when its theory dies. The Law of Arhat is not the Law of Buddha! Try to realize this!

Li Hongzhi
September 28, 1995

Constancy

With the master, you are full of confidence. Without the master, you seem to have lost zest in cultivation. It seems that you cultivate for the master and have come for the sake of zest. That is one great disadvantage of a person with average inborn qualities. Sakyamuni, Jesus, Lao Zi (Lao-tsu) and Confucius were gone for over two thousand years. However, their disciples have never felt that they have nothing to cultivate without their masters at their side. Cultivation practice is oneself's own business. No one can do it for you. As a master, he can only tell you the Law and principles on the surface. It is your own job to cultivate your heart, to abolish your desires, and to become awakened from illusions. If you have come for the sake of zest, you cannot be firm in mind. When entering the secular society, you are bound to forget the fundamental. If you do not firmly stick to your faith, you will gain nothing throughout your life. When will be the next lucky chance? It's really hard to say!

Li Hongzhi
October 6, 1995

Exposition Of Buddhism Is The Weakest And Smallest Portion Of Buddha Law

All living creatures! Never use Buddhism to measure the Great Law of Zhen Shan Ren (Truth Compassion Forbearance), because it is beyond measurement. People are accustomed to call the scriptures of Buddhism the Law. In fact, the Celestial Body is so vast that it is beyond the Buddha's understanding of the universe. Taiji (Taichi) of the Tao School is also only an understanding of the universe from the perspective of a small dimension. At the level of ordinary people there is no substantial Law except for a bit of phenomenon on the edge of the universe which can be used for cultivation. As ordinary people are human beings at the lowest level, they are not allowed to know the true Buddha Law. But people hear the sages say: showing respect to Buddha may bring one the lucky chance of cause and effect for cultivation in the future; practitioners who chant incantation may receive protection from intelligent beings; observing precepts may make one reach the standard of a practitioner. In history there have been people who tried to find out if what an enlightened being taught was Buddha Law. What the Tathagata Buddha said is the manifestation of Buddha-nature, or can be called the manifestation of the Law, but it was not the substantial Law of the universe, because in the past human beings were absolutely not allowed to know the true manifestation of Buddha Law. One cannot understand what Buddha Law is unless he has reached the high level through cultivation, therefore, mankind is even more kept in ignorance of the essence of real cultivation. For myriad ages

Falun Dafa for the first time has left the cosmic qualities (Buddha Law) to human beings. It is actually leaving them with a ladder by which they can ascend to Heavens. Hence, how can you use the old things of Buddhism to measure the Great Law of the universe?

Li Hongzhi
October 8, 1995

What Is Wisdom

People think celebrities, scholars and all sorts of specialists in human society are very great. In fact, they are very insignificant, because they are ordinary people. Their knowledge is merely that tiny bit recognized by the modern science of ordinary human society. In the vast universe, from the most macroscopic to the most microscopic, human society is exactly in the most middle, in the most outer layer, and on the very surface. The life in it is also in the lowest existing form, so its understanding of matter and spirit is also very little, superficial and pitiful. Even if one has mastered the knowledge of all humankind, he is still no more than an ordinary person.

Li Hongzhi
October 9, 1995

Not Work But Cultivation

Whether you can act according to the requirements I have laid down for the assistance centres to meet is a very important matter of principle, because it is concerned with the form of the future spread of the Law. Why can't you give up the habits you have developed long in the official circles? Don't take the assistance centre as an administrative body in ordinary human society and adopt its working methods and attitude towards it, such as issuing some documents, trying to carry out or implement something and urging people to deepen their understanding. A practitioner of the Great Law can only improve his Xinxing (mind-nature) and raise his achievement status and attainment level through cultivation. Sometimes, when a meeting is held, such a formula as used in the work unit of ordinary people is adopted. For example, a certain official will make a speech and a certain head will give a summary. Now even the state is trying to reform those corrupted practices and bureaucratic procedures in society. As a practitioner, you have known that humankind in the Period of Decline is no longer working in all aspects. Why do you still cling to the working methods that are most unfit for cultivation? We will never turn it into an administrative entity or an enterprise.

In past years there were some retired people who had nothing to do. They found Falun Dafa good and offered to come to work so as to replenish their unbearable void in their leisure time. It certainly won't do! Falun Dafa is for cultivating, not for working. All the working personnel in our cultivation system are first of all genuine practitioners with high Xinxing, who serve as models of cultivating Xinxing. We do not need ordinary-person types of leaders.

Li Hongzhi
October 12, 1995

Cultivating After Retirement

It's a great pity that some practitioners who have attended my lectures and have good inborn qualities no longer do cultivation because they are busy at work. If they were average ordinary people, I would say nothing more and leave them alone. But these people are promising. Human morality is sliding down the wrong road a thousand miles a day. Ordinary people are all drifting along with the current. The farther away you are from the Tao, the more difficult it will be for you to come back through cultivation. As a matter of fact, cultivation means cultivating the human mind. Especially in the complicated environment of your work unit, you will find it a good chance to improve your Xinxing (mind-nature). Once retired, haven't you lost the best environment for your cultivation? What can you cultivate when there are no conflicts? How can you improve yourself? The human life is limited. You may have a good plan, but how can you know that there will be enough time left for you to cultivate? Cultivation is not a child's play. It is more serious than any other business of ordinary people. It is not what you take it to be. Once you miss the chance, when will you get a human body again in going through the Sixfold Path of Transmigration? Opportunity knocks but once. Only when the illusion you hold on to has gone will you come to realize what you have lost.

Li Hongzhi
October 13, 1995

Law Right

When humans have no virtues, there will be natural calamities and man-made disasters. When the Earth has no virtues, myriad things will wither and fall. When Heaven does not follow the Tao, the ground will collapse, Heaven will fall and the firmament will be empty. When the Law is right, the universe will also be right. Bursting with vitality, Heaven and Earth will be stable, and the Law will exist forever.

Li Hongzhi
November 12, 1995

Saint

A saint, who carries out Heaven's decree in this world and Heaven above, possesses great virtues and is kindhearted, cherishes lofty aims and regards trivial matters, has an extensive knowledge of the principles of the Law and so can break illusions. He saves the people and benefits mankind, and therefore wins great merit naturally.

Li Hongzhi
November 17, 1995

Seeking The Discipleship With The Master

The Great Law is being promulgated far and wide. Those who have heard about it are looking for it. Those who have attained it are delighted with it. Practitioners are increasing day by day and they are countless. However, most self-learners have the intention of seeking the discipleship with the master and are worried that they will not receive the true essence if they do not see me in person, which, in fact, results from a superficial learning of the Law. The promulgation of the Law I am doing is a universal salvation. Whoever learns it is my disciple. I will not follow the old ceremony and convention. I only want to see your heart instead of any formality. What's the good of seeking the discipleship with the master if you do not practise the genuine cultivation? A genuine practitioner will gain naturally without seeking it. All cultivation energy and all Law are in the Book, and you will naturally attain them by reading through the Great Law. The learner will have a natural change, and he has already been in the Tao when he reads the Book over and over again. I will definitely have my Law-bodies to protect him without being noticed. If one perseveres in his cultivation, he will certainly complete the right achievement in future.

Li Hongzhi
December 8, 1995

An Explicit Direction

At present there is a very conspicuous problem, namely, some practitioners saw or came into contact with the space of a certain dimension when their True Spirits left their bodies. Feeling that was so splendid and everything actually existed, they did not want to come back, which resulted in the death of their physical bodies. So they just stayed in that realm and were not able to be back. But none of them are out of the Three Realms. I have talked about this problem before. Don't feels reluctant to leave a certain dimension during cultivation. Only when you have completed the whole course of your cultivation can you achieve the consummation. So you must come back no matter how good a place you have seen is when your True Spirit goes out.

There are still some practitioners who have a wrong understanding. They think that by practising Falun Dafa they have insured their life and their physical bodies will never die. Our cultivation system aims at cultivating both nature and life. A practitioner can prolong his life as he cultivates himself. However, some have not made enough efforts when they cultivate within the In-Triple-World-Law (Shi-Jian-Fa) and keep lingering in a level. When they reach a level with a great effort, they linger in that level again. Cultivation is a serious matter, so it is very difficult to guarantee someone from a natural death as predestined. However, there is no such problem in the cultivation beyond the In-Triple-World-Law, but the situation is quite complicated within the In-Triple-

World-Law.

Li Hongzhi
December 21, 1995

For Whom Do You Cultivate

When some people use the mass media to criticize qigong, some of the practitioners waver in determination and give up their cultivation. It seems to them as if those who make use of the media are more brilliant than Buddha Law, as if they cultivate for others. Some others are scared under the pressure and no longer do cultivation. Can this kind of people complete the right achievement? Are they going to betray the Buddha at the crucial moment? Isn't fear an attachment? Cultivation is something like great waves washing away the sand, and only what is left is the gold.

In fact, from ancient times to the present there has been a principle existing in human society, which is called inter-generation and inter-inhibition. So, where there is the good, there is the bad; where there is the right, there is the evil; where there is the virtuous, there is the wicked; where there are humans, there are ghosts; and where there are Buddhas, there are demons. This is even more so in human society. Where there is the positive, there is the negative; where there is avocation, there is objection; where there are believers, there are unbelievers; where there are good people, there are bad ones; where there are selfless people, there are selfish ones; and where there are people who can sacrifice their own interests for the sake of others, there are people who would stop at nothing to benefit themselves. This is the principle of the past. Therefore, if an individual, a collective or even a nation wants to accomplish a good deed, there will be some resistance of the equivalent force from the bad. Thus, one will not feel that it is an easy gain after he succeeds, and then he treasures it. This was always the way of development for mankind in the past (the principle of inter-generation and inter-inhibition are going to change in the future).

To talk about it from another aspect, cultivation is supernormal. No matter who he is, isn't his criticism of qigong the view of an ordinary person? Can he have the right to deny Buddha Law and cultivation? Can any organization of mankind be above the deity and Buddha? Can the critic of qigong have the capability of commanding the Buddha? He says the Buddha is not good, is the Buddha really not good? He says there is no Buddha, is there really no Buddha? The disaster of the Law during the Great Cultural Revolution resulted from the changes of the entire cosmic climate. Buddhas, Tao and Gods all followed the will of Heaven. The disaster of the Law was actually the disaster of human beings and the disaster of religion, but not the disaster of Buddhas.

The fundamental cause for the destruction of the religion is the corruption of the human mind. People worshiping the Buddha is no longer for the cultivation of Buddhahood, but for the blessings of the Buddha so that they can make a fortune, eliminate misfortune, have a son or lead a free and easy life. Everybody made much karma in his prior lives. How can he be free and comfortable? How is it possible for him not to pay his karmic debts for his wrong-doings? Seeing the human mind not right, the demons came out of their caves one after another to disrupt the human world with disasters. Finding the human mind not right, the deities and Buddhas left their positions one after another by abandoning the temples. Many foxes, yellow-weasels, ghosts and snakes were brought into the temples by people who were after wealth and gain. Should such temples not be smashed? It is the fault of the common people. The reason why the Buddhas do not condemn the people is that people all rest in fallacies and they have already done harm to themselves. Besides, they have made tremendous karma for themselves and before long there will be great disasters awaiting them. What's the necessity of punishing them? In fact, people will suffer retribution sometime in the future for their wrong-doings, they just neither awake to it nor believe it. When they meet with a mishap, they think it is accidental.

When a person or a social force, no matter who he is or what it is, does not want you to cultivate, then you will drop your cultivation. Do you cultivate for them? Will they give you the right achievement? Don't you have blind faith in them when you incline towards them? Actually, this is simply a folly! Besides, what we practise is not qigong but the cultivation of Buddha Law. Isn't any pressure a fundamental test of your determination to cultivate Buddha Law? If you are not steadfast to the Law at all, then everything else is out of the question.

Li Hongzhi

December 21, 1995

Terms Of Buddha Law

As some practitioners were once lay Buddhists, they have a deep impression of the terms used in Buddhist scriptures. When these practitioners find that there are terms identical with Buddhism in my words, they think these terms have the same meaning as the terms of Buddhism. In fact, they do not mean exactly the same. Some terms of Buddhism in the Han region are Chinese vocabulary, not absolute Buddhist terminology.

The crux is that these practitioners are always unwilling to give up the things of Buddhism because they have not realized that the impression of Buddhism still works in their minds and do not have a deep enough understanding of cultivating the one and only way. In fact, doesn't that identical understanding mean interference? If you have misrepresented my meaning, haven't you gone to the cultivation of Buddhism?

Li Hongzhi
December 21, 1995

Pacifying The External
By Cultivating The Internal

If humans pay no attention to virtue, there will be great disorder beyond control under heaven; people will be close enemies of each other and live without happiness. When people live without happiness, they are not afraid to die. Just as Lao Zi (Lao-tsu) said, "If men fear no death, how could you threaten them with death?" This is a great threat imminent. Peace under heaven is what people desire. If more laws and decrees are promulgated to attain stability at this time, it will only lead to the opposite. To solve the problem, a permanent remedy can only be found in the universal cultivation of virtue. If officials are unselfish, the state will not be corrupted. If people lay stress on self-cultivation and nurture of their virtues and both administrators and civilians exercise self-restraint on their minds, then the whole nation will be stable and quiet. This accords with the feelings of the people everywhere. The kingdom will become impregnable, and foreign aggressors will naturally feel too fearful to attack, thus peace will reign under heaven. This is done by a Saint.

Li Hongzhi
January 5, 1996

Further Giving Up Attachments

My disciples! It is of no use for me to be anxious! Why can't you let go of that heart of an ordinary person? Why are you reluctant to make a further step forward? Our practitioners, including our working staff, even if for the work of the Great Law, are jealous of each other. Can you attain Buddhahood like this? I want to have a loose administration simply because you cling to ordinary people and thus will lose your mental balance in your work. The Great Law belongs to the whole universe, not to an insignificant person. Whoever does the job is spreading the Great Law. Why care about whether it should be done by you or by me? Do you intend to bring this attachment along with you to the paradise to contend with the Buddha if you do not let it go? Nobody has the ability to take on the Great Law. Give up your unbalanced psychology! When you feel something unbearable, isn't it caused by your attachment? Our practitioners, do not feel that you are not included! I hope all of you should make an examination of yourselves, because all of you, except me, Li Hongzhi, are practitioners. Think it over, why do I promulgate such a great Law in the Last Havoc? If I reveal the real truth to you, I am actually teaching an evil way, because in that case learners of the Law would definitely come to learn the Law for that. This is the learning of the Law with desires. The only way to save people is to make them seek for the right so as to let go of their attachments. You all know that you will not succeed in your cultivation if you do not let go of your attachments. Why don't you have the courage to give a further abandonment of them and make a further step forward? In fact, there must be an unspeakable reason for my promulgation of the Great Law. Once the truth presents itself, you will find it too late for regrets. I have seen some of your hearts, but I cannot tell you directly. If I told you, you would keep your master's words in mind and be attached to them all your life. I wouldn't like to ruin even one of my disciples. It is very difficult to save people, but it is even more difficult to get awakened. It is important that every one of you should regard yourself as one in it and try to awake to it. You all know that the Great Law is good, then, why can't you let go of your attachments?

Li Hongzhi
January 6, 1996

Verification

Buddha Law can save people, but it is not for the salvation of people that Buddha Law has come into existence. Buddha Law can reveal the mysteries of the universe, life, and science, and can make humankind take a correct road of science again, but it is not for the guidance of human science that Buddha Law has been brought forth.

Buddha Law is cosmic qualities. It is the factor that has brought up the source of matter, and the cause for the formation of the universe.

Then there will be many specialists and scholars who will have their wisdom opened in Buddha Law in future. They will become pioneers in different areas of learning of the new humankind. However, it is not to have you become a pioneer that Buddha Law has given you the wisdom. You have got it simply because you are a practitioner. That is to say, you are first of all a practitioner, and then a specialist. As a practitioner, you should make use of all favourable conditions to spread the Great Law and prove that the Great Law is correct, is the real science, not a sermon or idealism, which is the obligation of every practitioner. Without this great Buddha Law, there would be nothing existing in the universe, including everything from the most macroscopic to the most microscopic, and all the knowledge of ordinary human society.

Li Hongzhi
January 8, 1996

A Practitioner Can Always Find Himself In It

As a practitioner, all the vexations he encounters among ordinary people are ordeals for him to go through, and all the praises he receives are tests for him to pass.

Li Hongzhi
January 14, 1996

What Is Ren

Ren (Forbearance) is the key to improve one's Xinxing . To endure with hatred, grievances or tears is the Ren of an ordinary person who is attached to his misgivings. To bear without any hatred or grievances at all is the Ren of a practitioner.

Li Hongzhi
January 21, 1996

What Is Superstition

Contemporary Chinese would turn pale at the mere mention of the term superstition because many people call whatever they don't believe superstition. In fact, the two characters "mi-xin" (superstition), which was covered with an ultra-"leftist" cloak during the "Great Cultural Revolution", was the strongest term of destruction to the then national culture and the most horrible "big hat", and therefore, it has become the most irresponsible pet phrase of those who are simple-minded and obstinate. As for those who claim to be the so-called materialists, they call superstition whatever is beyond their knowledge or beyond the recognition of science. If people were to understand things according to this theory, humankind would not make any more progress nor would science develop any more, because the new development and discovery of science are all beyond the recognition of our predecessors. Don't these people practise idealism themselves, then? Once people believe something, aren't they fascinated about it? Isn't it superstition for some people to have faith in modern science or modern medicine? And isn't it superstition for people to worship idols? Actually, the word superstition is a very common term. Once people have faith in something, including truth, that is superstition which carries no derogatory sense. However, a connotation suggestive of the so-called "feudal" has been put into it by those with ulterior motives when they make attacks on others. Thus it has become a demagogic term with fighting power which can be used all the more to incite the simple-minded people to follow suit.

As a matter of fact, the term "superstition" should not have been used in this way and the imposed connotation does not exist, either. What the two characters mi-xin (superstition) suggests is not a bad thing. If soldiers do not have faith in discipline, they will not have fighting power; if students do not have faith in their schools and teachers, they will not gain knowledge; if children do not have faith in their parents, they will not be well brought up; if people do not have faith in their careers, they will not do their work well. If humankind has no belief, they will have no moral standards, and then the human heart will lose good intentions and be occupied by evil thoughts. Humankind of this time will suffer a sharp decline in morality, and with their evil thoughts in command, they will treat each other as close enemies and stop at no evil to gratify their selfish desires. However, the bad people who have imposed a negative connotation on the two characters mi-xin (superstition) have achieved their aim, though, it is very likely that they will have ruined humankind in the matter of human nature.

Li Hongzhi
January 22, 1996
Revised on August 29, 1996

Disease-Karma

Why does a new practitioner who is at the initial stage of learning the cultivation system and an old practitioner whose body has been adjusted, feel unwell in cultivation as if they were suffering from a serious illness? And why does this happen periodically? When lecturing on the Law, I told you that it indicated your karma was being eliminated, and that your enlightenment quality would be also improved when your karma accumulated in your previous lives was abolished. You were also tested in your determination of cultivating the Great Law until you were out of the cultivation of the In-Triple-World-Law (Shi-Jian-Fa). This is said in a broad sense.

As a matter of fact, a human being has so many previous existences that are countless, and he made a lot of karma in each existence. When he is reincarnated, a part of his disease-karma has been pressed into the microscopic composition deep in his body. When he is born, the physical body of the new surface matter has no disease-karma (but exceptions also occur for those who have tremendous karma). Well, what was pressed into the body in the last existence will return outward, and when it comes to the surface physical body, the person will become ill. However, more often than not there will be an external cause in the surface material world which touches off his disease. Thus, it conforms to the objective laws of our surface material world, in other words, it accords with the principles of this world. As a consequence, ordinary people are kept in the dark about the real cause of the illness and are lost in illusions without trying to understand it. But when one is ill, he will take medicine or try to cure the disease by various means. By doing so, he has actually pressed the disease deep into the body again. As a result, before he has paid his karmic debt for his disease, which results from the wrong-doings he did in his last existence, he will do some bad things to harm other people in this existence and suffer from various diseases with the new disease-karma he has made. However, by taking medicine or adopting various therapies, one has pressed the disease deep into the body again. Operation can do nothing but to excise some flesh from the body in the surface material space, while the disease-karma in another space has not been removed at all. It is simply beyond the reach of modern medical technology. When one suffers from a disease again, he will take another treatment. When he is reincarnated again after his death, the disease-karma, if there is any, will be pressed deep into his body again. With the repetition of this process in endless cycles, and after a long stream of one's existences, there is infinite disease-karma left in his body. Therefore, I say that people today are born with karma built upon karma. Besides disease-karma, they have other kinds of karma. Therefore people would have hardships, sufferings and troubles in their life. How is it possible for them to seek happiness without paying their karmic debts? People nowadays have so much karma that they are soaked in it at all times and in all situations, and at all times and in all situations they may meet with mishaps. Whenever they leave the house, there will be something bad waiting for them. But people do not tolerate others when they are in conflict. Not knowing that they are paying their karmic debts owed in the past, they may treat you worse if you are bad to them. They make new karma before they pay up the old ones, which makes public morality decline day by day and each person is treating another as a close enemy. There are also many people who cannot understand the phenomenon: What is wrong with people today? What is wrong with the society today? If humankind goes on like this, they will be in danger!

As for practitioners, your master will eliminate a part of your karma, but you yourselves also have to repay a part. So you will feel unwell as if you were suffering from a disease. Cultivation means that you will be cleaned up from the origin of your life. The human body is like a tree with annual rings, disease-karma existing in each layer of your body. So your body has to be cleaned up from the very centre. But you could not stand it if all the karma was pushed out all at once and your life would be in danger. Therefore, only one or two may be pushed out at regular intervals so that you can cope with it and repay your karma during your suffering, yet it is only the bit left for you to endure yourselves after I have removed the karma for you. Only when you reach the highest form of the In-Triple-World-Law and attain the pure-white body through cultivation will all of your karma be pushed out. But there are also some people who have very little disease-karma and there may exist other special cases. The cultivation of the Beyond-Triple-World-Law means the cultivation of the purest Arhat-body without any disease-karma. However, if one has not yet achieved the consummation and is still in cultivation to a higher level when he is beyond the cultivation of the In-Triple-World-Law, he may still have sufferings, tribulations, and some ordeals for him to go through in order to raise his level. But he is merely to manage person-to-person and person-to-affair Xinxing conflicts, and further let go of attachments, but he does not have any disease-karma in his body.

As for the matter of eliminating the disease-karma, nobody can do it causally for an ordinary person. There is no possibility of doing so at all for an ordinary person who does not cultivate. An ordinary person can only depend on medical treatment. Doing this casually for an ordinary person is actually going against the heavenly principles. That is to say, one can do evil without having to repay his karma. It absolutely does not work if one does not pay his debts. It is not permitted by Heaven's laws! Even by means of the general qigong therapy, it is the same to heal the sickness by pressing the karma deep into his body. When a person has too much karma and is still doing evil, he will be annihilated and meet with the perdition, complete destruction of both body and spirit at his death. A great enlightened being can thoroughly eliminate the origin of the disease-karma when he heals the illness, but he will do so with a purpose. The main aim is to save the people.

Li Hongzhi
March 10, 1996

Practitioners' Taboo

Those who are attached to fame are actually practising an evil way artificially. When they try to establish a reputation in this world, they will certainly say good and mean evil, and therefore mislead people by disrupting the Law.

Those who are attached to money are actually seeking wealth and doing sham cultivation. Such people will spoil Buddha's teachings and the Law. They are in fact idling away their lives, not cultivating Buddhahood.

Those who are attached to lust are not different from the wicked. When chanting the scripture, they even cast furtive glances. Such people are very far away from the Tao and are wicked ordinary people.

Those who are attached to the affection for their kinsfolk will definitely be worn out by, pestered with and tormented by such an affection. Such people seize the thread of affection and let it tie themselves up for their whole life. When reaching old age, they will find it too late to repent.

Li Hongzhi
April 15, 1996

Perfect Harmony

(I)

People vary from person to person in the matter of taking life as they work in their respective environment. So does the balance of life vary in manifestations. As a practitioner, you should first of all let go of all attachments and conform to the social state of ordinary human society, which is also the performance of protecting the Law of a dimension. If nobody undertakes the human jobs, then the Law of this dimension will not exist.

(II)

Life in the Law will live or die naturally. The universe goes through formation, existence and destruction, and humans have birth, old age, disease and death. There also, meanwhile, exist unnatural births or deaths for the balance of life. Ren (forbearance) includes loss, while a complete abandonment is a higher principle of non-omission.

Li Hongzhi
April 19, 1996

Non-omission

Ren (forbearance) includes giving. Being able to give is sublimation of one's cultivation. The Law has different levels. A practitioner's understanding of the Law is his understanding of the Law at a particular level he has reached through cultivation. The reason why different practitioners have different understandings of the Law is that they are at different levels.

The Law has different requirements for the practitioners at different levels. Giving is the manifestation of one's abandonment of attachments of an ordinary person. If one can really give up unperturbedly with his heart remaining unmoved, he is actually at that level already. Cultivating yourself is for the purpose of improving yourself, though. Since you can give up the attachment, why not give up the fear of attachment itself too? Isn't it a further abandonment to give up everything for the attainment of non-omission? However, if a practitioner or an ordinary person, who is even unable to make fundamental abandonment, also talks about this principle, he is actually disrupting the Law by making an excuse for the attachment he will not let go of.

Li Hongzhi
April 26, 1996

Cultivation And Work

With the exception of the professional ones in temples, the vast majority of our disciples of Falun Dafa cultivate themselves in ordinary human society. Having learnt and practised the Great Law, they can all care less of fame and interest. However, a shallow understanding of the Law has aroused a problem: some few of the disciples gave up their jobs in ordinary human society or refused to take up the position when they were promoted, which has caused many unnecessary interference in their work and life, therefore has directly affected their cultivation. There were also some disciples engaged in legitimate business, who also gave up their business thinking that they cared little about money and their business would harm others and affect their own cultivation.

In fact, the inner meanings of the Great Law are very profound. Letting go of an ordinary person's mind does not mean giving up an ordinary person's job. Letting go of fame and interest is not separating yourself from ordinary human society. I have repeatedly pointed out that: those who cultivate in ordinary human society shall conform to the state of ordinary human society.

From another point of view, if all the positions of leadership in ordinary human society were taken up by the people like us who can let go of their personal fame and interest, what a great advantage would it bring to the people? And what would it bring to society if they were taken up by those with insatiable greed? If business people were practitioners of the Great Law, what would the current tendencies of society be like?

The Great Law of the universe (Buddha Law) is complete and is linked from the highest to the lowest level. You should know that ordinary human society is also a composition of the Law of a level. If everybody learned the Great Law and gave up their jobs, then ordinary human society would not exist and the Law of this level would not exist. Ordinary human society is also the manifestation of Buddha Law at the lowest level and the existing form of life and matter of Buddha Law at this level.

Li Hongzhi
April 26, 1996

Correction

At present, practitioners in different parts of the country take the following sayings suggested by the Research Society

"Reading the Great Law intensively,

Cultivating your Xinxing sincerely, and

Practising the movements painstakingly..." etc.

as the Law or my words to spread and to learn. In fact, they are neither my words, nor have a deeper inner meaning, and still less are the Law. What is meant by reading intensively differs greatly from my requirement of the learning of the Law. As a matter of fact, I was quite explicit about reading the books in *Learning the Law* I wrote on September 9, 1995, and the implication of intensive reading has interfered in *Learning the Law* severely. From now on you shall pay attention to the gravity of this problem. I have talked about the reason why Buddhism was lost in India and the lesson it taught us. If care is not taken in future, there will begin to arise the disruption of the Law. Mind: don't try to ascertain where the responsibility lies when a problem crops up. Try to think about your own conduct. It is also unnecessary to find out who wrote them. Take a lesson from it and be careful in future.

Li Hongzhi
April 28, 1996

Diamond

To keep the Great Law unchanged forever, it seems that there still exists a problem: there are always such practitioners who, prompted by the attachment to show-off and the intention of creating something new and original, will do something to interfere with the Great Law when they have an opportunity, which can be very grave sometimes. For example, recently there was someone saying that I taught a certain practitioner the essentials of the movements alone (as a matter of fact, I only corrected his movements when the practitioner asked me), thus denying the movements I have been imparting in different areas for the past few years and openly altering the exercises of the Great Law when I am still here in this world and, the video tape for teaching the exercises is still in circulation. He told the practitioners not to perform the movements according to the video tape but to follow his way, saying that the teacher has high cultivation energy and he is different from his students and the like, and telling the practitioners to perform the movements according to their own conditions first and then gradually come to the correct performance and so on and so forth.

I teach the exercises in one step for fear that the practitioners may make an arbitrary alteration to them. Once the mechanism is formed, it can never be altered. The matter seems quite trivial, but in reality it is the start of severe disruption of the Law. Some other people take the transition movements as independent ones and tell the practitioners to perform them in a standardized way. By doing so, they are just trying to be different. Now this has had a serious influence in various areas. My disciples! Why do you follow them rashly when the video tape for teaching the exercises with my demonstration is still available?! The Great Law is the solemn Great Law of the universe. Even if you disrupt a bit of it, what a great sin you have committed! As a practitioner, you should cultivate yourself in an open and decent manner and concentrate on the key points. How can it be possible that everyone performs the movements exactly in the same way without any differences? Don't concentrate on such trivialities. The exercises are a form to help you to achieve the consummation, which are important nevertheless, but don't dig into the tip of a horn. You should devote more time and energy to the improvement of your Xinxing. In fact, more often than not, the interference in the Great Law comes from within ourselves. The external factors can only affect some few individuals but they cannot change the Law. Whether at present or in future, those who is able to disrupt our Law will be nobody but the practitioners within our cultivation system. Do be careful! Our Law is indestructible like diamond. No one can use any excuse to alter even a bit of the movements with which we are to achieve the consummation for any reason or under any circumstances. Otherwise, no matter whether he has a good motive or not, he is disrupting the Law.

Li Hongzhi
May 11, 1996

Never Talk Wildly

There has been an expression recently. When practitioners spread the Great Law and lead some people with predestined relationship to attain the Law and take the road of cultivation, some of you may say that you have saved people such as "I have saved several people today, how many people have you saved?" and so on. Actually, it is the Law that saves the people, and it is only the master who can do such a thing. You have no more than led the people with predestined relationship to attain of the Law. Whether they can really be saved or not has also to depend on their capability of achieving the consummation through cultivation. Do be careful: intentional or unintentional big talks will even shock a Buddha. Don't create obstacles for your cultivation. You must also cultivate your speech (Xiu Kou) in this respect. I hope you can understand.

Li Hongzhi
May 21, 1996

Alarmed Awakening

The time for genuine cultivation of the Great Law is limited. Many practitioners have realized that they should make the best use of their time and are making further advances incessantly. However, there are some practitioners who don't know how to value their time and bother their heads about something that is unnecessary for them to bother about. Since the Great Law *Zhuan Falun* was printed, many people have compared the recordings of my lectures on the Law with the Book, saying the Research Society has changed the teacher's words; others say that the Book was written with the help of so-and-so, thus disrupting the Law. Now I tell you, the Great Law is that of mine, Li Hongzhi's Law. The Law I have promulgated to save you was uttered from my very mouth, and when lecturing on the Law I used no text of speech or material but only a piece of paper on which there were no more than a few issues that were quite simple but not understandable to others to remind me what to speak to my students each day. Each time I lectured on the Law, I presented it from a different angle and delivered my speech according to the students' receptivity. Therefore, whenever I lectured on the Law, I would talk about the same issue from a different angle. What's more, the Law of this Book are the cosmic qualities, and it is the true manifestation of the great Buddha Law. It is the primordial belongings of my own that came back to my mind after I attained enlightenment through cultivation. I have spoken it out with the language of ordinary people and promulgated it to you and those in heaven to put the universe right with the Law. For the convenience of your cultivation, I assigned some students to take down the content of my lectures from the tape recordings without changing anything about my original words before they handed it in for me to make revisions. The students merely copied what I had revised again or typed it with a computer so that I could make further revisions. As far as *Zhuan Falun* is concerned, I finalized the manuscript by making three revisions myself before it was published.

Nobody else has ever changed a bit of the content and meaning of this book of the Great Law. Who can possibly do it? There are three reasons for its difference from the tape recordings: first, I made revisions on a combination of many of my lectures on the Law to facilitate the practitioners' cultivation. Second, I lectured on the Law according to the different receptivity of the students and the then situation and environment, and therefore I had to make a change in the language and the grammatical structures when I rearranged it into a book. Third, misunderstandings may occur when practitioners read the written form of the lectures, so the language needs to be modified, but it still retains the state and colloquialism in which I lectured on the Law. *Zhuan Falun (Volume Two)* and *Exposition of Falun Dafa* were also revised entirely by myself before they were published. I wrote *Zhuan Falun (Volume Two)* in different modes of thinking at different levels, so some people find different styles of writing in it and don't quite understand. These indeed are not things of ordinary people. In fact, *Volume Two* is to be left for future generations to see to what extent humankind has become corrupt today, and thus a profound lesson is left in history for people to learn, while *China Falun Gong*, including its revised version, is only something interim in the form of qigong for people to understand at the beginning of promulgation of the Law.

The disruption of the Law takes many forms, of which unintentional disruption by disciples within the cultivation way is most difficult to be perceived. The Decline of Sakyamuni's Buddhism began just in this way and the lesson is profound.

Disciples, do remember: all the scriptures of Falun Dafa are the Law lectured on by me, and they were revised and rearranged by myself. From now on, none of you may take excerpts from the tape recordings of my lectures on the Law or rearrange them for written material. Whatever excuses you may make, including the so-called contrast of the differences between the speech and its written form and so on, you are disrupting the Law.

The changes of the Celestial Body and the development of mankind are not accidental. The trends of human society are the arrangements of history and they occur with the movements of the celestial phenomena. In future there will be more people in the world learning the Great Law. This is not what anyone can do on the impulse of the moment when he wants to. Can it be possible that there are no arrangements in every aspect in history for such a great event? Actually, whatever I have done was all well-arranged countless years ago, including those who have attained the Law. Nothing is accidental, but the manifestations are the same as those of ordinary people. As a matter of fact, what my masters for this existence of mine have imparted to me is something I had arranged for them to attain a number of existences ago so that I could have them impart it back to me again on the occasion predestined to enlighten me about the entirety of my Law.

Therefore, I tell you that not only the human beings at this level but also the higher dimensions are all learning this Law. The rectification of the Law has begun because a very large sphere of the Celestial Body has deviated from the cosmic qualities. Humankind does not matter in the vast universe. The Earth is nothing but a grain of cosmic dust. If human beings want to be valued by intelligent beings, they have no choice but to cultivate themselves and become intelligent beings, too!

Li Hongzhi
May 27, 1996

Fixity Of The Law

Over the past two years there have appeared some problems among the practitioners in their cultivation, and I have been also watching their cultivation. In order to promptly deal with the problem that has appeared, I often write some short articles on purpose (the practitioners call them scriptures) to direct them in their cultivation, which is aimed at leaving a stable, healthy and correct way of cultivating the Great Law for future generations. For generation after generation, only when people follow the way I personally have left for them in their cultivation can they achieve the consummation.

However, recently I saw a copy of material at a practice site in Hong Kong, which had been passed on there from another part of the country. There were two short articles in the material, which I did not want to have published. This was a serious and intentional disruption of the Great Law! It is not right, either, to have taken them down from the tape recordings and rearranged them without permission. I have made it clear in *Alarmed Awakening* that nobody is allowed to take my words down from the tape recordings and rearrange them for written material under any excuses. Whoever does so is disrupting the Law. Besides, I keep stressing the point that you cannot pass the notes you made yourselves during my lectures among others. Why do you still do that? What heart prompted you to write them? I tell you that, with the exception of the several books of mine which have been formally published and my signed and dated short articles which have been distributed to different parts of the country by the Research Society, all that has been rearranged without permission is disrupting the Law. Cultivation is your own business, and it is up to you what to seek. An ordinary person has both demon-nature and Buddha-nature. Once his thinking is not right, his demon-nature will begin to function. I tell you once again that outsiders can never disrupt the Law. Those who can disrupt the Law will be none but the practitioners within our cultivation system. Do remember!

Every step I, Li Hongzhi, take is for the unchangeable and indestructible form established for the promulgation of the Great Law to future generations. Such a Great Law is not something done on the impulse of the moment. Never for aeons can a bit of deviation be permitted. Starting to safeguard the Great Law from oneself is forever the responsibility of the disciples of the Great Law likewise, because it belongs to sentient beings of the universe, among whom you are included.

Li Hongzhi
June 11, 1996

Cultivation And Responsibility

Cultivating in earnest and making further advances are for the purpose of achieving the consummation as soon as possible. A practitioner is one who tries to get rid of the attachments of ordinary people. Disciples, you must know what you are doing yourselves!

To be responsible to the Great Law, the assistance centres and general assistance centres in different parts of the country, and the Research Society are entitled to replace any assistant or head of a branch. So a person in charge may be replaced in the light of the different conditions sometimes. As a person in charge is first of all a practitioner who is to cultivate himself and not to serve as the head, he should be ready to take a lower as well as a higher post. Serving as a person in charge is for the sake of cultivation. Not serving as a person in charge is cultivation likewise. If the person replaced takes it to heart, isn't it his attachment that is working? Isn't it a good opportunity for him to give up that attachment? So, still not being able to let go of that attachment truly justifies the replacement. An attachment to serving as a person in charge itself is just an impure motive for cultivation. Therefore, my disciples! I have to remind you that it is impossible for you to achieve the consummation if you do not give up this attachment.

Li Hongzhi
June 12, 1996

Disposal Of Handwritten Copies Of Scriptures

At present, more and more people are learning the Great Law, and the number of new practitioners doubles and redoubles each week. As our publishing house has not yet published enough books, and the supply does not meet the demand, it is difficult for people to buy them in some areas or villages. Some practitioners asked me what to do with their handwritten copies of the Great Law. I tell you that for the time being you can give your handwritten copies of *Zhuan Falun* or other scriptures when you were learning the Great Law to the people who are going to the rural areas to spread the cultivation system and the Great Law and ask them to take the copies to the farmers. At the same time, this can lessen their economic burden. Therefore, it is required that the handwriting of the practitioners' handwritten copies should be neat so that the farmers with little education can understand them. And handwritten copies have the same power of the Law as printed books.

Li Hongzhi
June 26, 1996

Law Assembly

It is quite necessary for the disciples to have a mutual exchange of what they feel or what they have learned and what they awake to in cultivation. It is no problem for them to help each other and improve themselves together as long as they have no intention of showing off. In order to give an impetus to the spread of the Great Law, some assemblies for the exchange of cultivation experience have been held in different areas. These assemblies are all very good and healthy both in form and content. Nevertheless, the practitioners' speech scripts must be examined and approved by the Assistance Centre beforehand lest there should arise a problem in politics which has nothing to do with cultivation or the problem of incorrect guidance of cultivation and society. Meanwhile, the practitioners should also try to avoid practising the flashy and superficial boasting and exaggeration, which has been developed in theoretical study among ordinary people. They are not allowed to deliver a speech of a written text to be organized as if it is some material to be reported to a higher body with the show-off intention of self-expression.

A large-scale assembly for the exchange of cultivation experience sponsored by the General Assistance Centres at the provincial or municipal level should not be nation wide. A national or international one shall be sponsored by the General Society, and it should not be held too frequently. It would be better to have it once a year except for special cases. Be sure not to fall into a mere formality or get into competition with others, but organize it into a Law assembly that can really give an impetus to cultivation.

Li Hongzhi
June 26, 1996

A Letter To Dafa Shijiazhuang
General Assistance Centre

Dafa Shijiazhuang General Assistance Centre,

I know that your assembly for the exchange of cultivation experience was blocked. There are three reasons for this, and you will certainly draw useful lessons from them. In fact, this incident has directly affected the activities of the Great Law practitioners in Beijing and even in the other parts of the country, which has a certain negative effect on future normal activities of the Great Law. I think you will certainly realize this and do better in future.

I would like to say a few words more about Jing Zhanyi's public speeches. Jing Zhanyi's case is for the purpose of proving the scientific nature of the Great Law from the aspect of science so that the people in scientific, technological and academic circles can understand the Great Law. But we do not want Jing to make speeches to the practitioners, because such speeches will do them no good. They can only arouse the attachment of a novice practitioner or a disciple who does not learn the Law in earnest, while a disciple who learns the Law well will resolutely cultivate the Great Law as before without having to listen to such speeches.

Here is a more important point: I have promulgated the Law for two years and given my disciples two years' time for genuine cultivation. Within these two years of their genuine cultivation, I do not allow any activities that have nothing to do with genuine cultivation to interfere in an orderly process of improvement arranged step by step for the practitioners. If the speech is not given to scientific and academic circles to prove the scientific nature of the Great Law, but to the practitioners who have limited time for cultivation, just think about it, can there be a greater disturbance to the practitioners than this? In order to keep the practitioners from being disturbed, I even do not see them. If they see me, they may not calm down at least for several days, which would thus disrupt the order I have had my Law-bodies arranged for them. I talked it over to the Research Society, but perhaps it was not made clear to Jing Zhanyi. The matter is over, but don't try to ascertain where the responsibility lies. I think the main reason is that you do not understand it. But you must pay attention to it from now on. Everything we do today is to lay a foundation for future spreading of the Great Law for generation after generation throughout the ages so that a complete, correct and errorless cultivation form can pass down. Today I point this out not to criticize someone, but to rectify the cultivation form and to leave it for future generations.

This letter is to be copied to all the assistance centres.

Li Hongzhi
June 26, 1996

Rectification Of Nature

With the deepening of cultivation of the Great Law in earnest, many disciples have successively attained enlightenment or entered into gradual enlightenment, and they can see the real, magnificent, splendid and wonderful scenes in other spaces. The disciples who are becoming enlightened are so excited that they call my Law-body the second master or take my Law-body as a true and independent master. This is due to a wrong understanding. The Law-body is the manifestation of my omnipresent image of wisdom, but not an independent living entity. Some disciples even call Falun "Master Falun". This is absolutely wrong. Falun is another manifestation of the peculiarity of my Law-potency and the wisdom of the Great Law, which is too wonderful for words. It is the manifestation of the Law-nature of all matters in the universe from the macroscopic to the microscopic, not an independent being, either.

Disciples, do remember: do not try to understand or compliment my Law-bodies or Falun with the mind of an ordinary person when you see my Law-bodies and Falun accomplish those great, miraculous and magnificent things for you, because such a mind is a tangled expression of extremely poor enlightenment quality and Xinxing. As a matter of fact, all the forms of manifestations are concrete embodiments of my rectification of the Law and salvation of the people with my immensely powerful Law-potency.

Li Hongzhi
July 2, 1996

A Brief Talk On Shan

Shan is the expression of the cosmic qualities at different levels and in different spaces. It is also the basic nature of great enlightened beings. Therefore, a practitioner must cultivate Shan and become assimilated to Zhen Shan Ren (Truth Compassion Forbearance), the cosmic qualities. The vast Celestial Body was born of the cosmic qualities, Zhen Shan Ren. The promulgation of the Great Law is what it provides the living beings of the universe with the reappearance of their primordial historical nature. The Great Law is perfecting and harmonizing. Each word of the three characters Zhen Shan Ren also has cosmic qualities of Zhen Shan Ren. This is because matter is composed of microscopic substances and the microscopic matter is made up of more microscopic substances, which will go on and on until the infinitude. Therefore, Zhen is formed of Zhen Shan Ren, Shan is formed of Zhen Shan Ren, and Ren is formed of Zhen Shan Ren as well. The cultivation of Zhen by the Tao School is no other than the cultivation of Zhen Shan Ren, while the cultivation of Shan by the Buddha School is no other than the cultivation of Zhen Shan Ren again. In fact, they are different simply in superficial form.

When it comes to Shan, which is reflected in ordinary human society, some ordinary people who are very attached to ordinary human society may raise such a social question, saying: If people all learn the Great Law and all practise Shan, what shall we do when foreign aggressors launch a war against us? In fact, I have already stated in *Zhuan Falun* that the development of human society is brought about by the evolution of the celestial phenomena. Is a war of mankind, then, an accidental phenomenon? An area with huge karma and with corrupted human hearts is truly unstable. If a nation is really virtuous, it must have little karma, and never will a war come to it, because the principle of the Great Law does not allow it to happen and the cosmic qualities restrict everything. There is no need for people to worry that a virtuous nation will be invaded. The cosmic qualities -- the Great Law is present everywhere, spreading over the whole Celestial Body from the macroscopic to the microscopic. As to the Great Law I promulgate today, I pass it down not only to the Orientals, but to the Occidentals as well. Those good people among them should also be saved. All the nations that are to enter into the next new historical era will attain the Law and improve as a whole. It is not a question of one nation. The moral standards of humankind will also return to the original human nature.

Li Hongzhi
July 20, 1996

Annotation On The Rectification Of Nature

After I said "the Law-body and Falun are not independent living entities", some practitioners asked if it was contradictory to the statement given in *Zhuan Falun*: "The Law-body's consciousness and the Law-body's thoughts are controlled by the person. However, the Law-body itself is also an complete, independent, and realistic individual life." I think this is due to a poor understanding of the Law. The Law-bodies cannot be regarded as a concept of completely independent lives, because they are a wishful manifestation of the Law potency and wisdom of the image and thought of the master person. They have the ability to do anything independently according to the master person's intentions. The practitioners only noticed the second sentence without paying attention to the first one: "The Law-body's consciousness and the Law-body's thoughts are controlled by the person." So the Law-body has the traits of the master person's nature as well as the independent and integrated image of the master person, and can also accomplish independently all that the master person wants to do. While, ordinary lives are under nobody's control. When people see the Law-body, they will find it is a complete, independent and realistic individual life. In plain words, my Law-body is simply me, myself.

Li Hongzhi
July 21, 1996

70

Buddha-Nature Vs. Demon-Nature

In a very high, very microscopic space of the universe exist two different kinds of matter. They are also the two existing forms of matter, which are the manifestations of the supreme cosmic qualities, Zhen Shan Ren (Truth Compassion Forbearance) in a certain space dimension of the universe, penetrating to a certain space from top to bottom and from the macroscopic to the microscopic. As the Law manifests in its state from dimension to dimension, the further down the matter of two properties is, the more they differ in manifestations, and the more difference there is between them. Thus there comes into existence what the Tao School practices, the theory of Yin-Yang and Taiji (Taichi). Further down again, the matter of two different properties is getting more and more opposite to each other. Hence it forms the principle of inter-generation and inter-inhibition.

With inter-generation and inter-inhibition there simply appear the virtuous and the wicked, the righteous and the evil, and the good and the bad. Reflected in life, in this way, where there are Buddhas, there are demons, and where there are humans, there are ghosts. It becomes all the more noticeable and complex in ordinary human society. Where there are good people, there are bad ones; where there are selfless people, there are selfish ones; where there are broad-minded people, there are narrow-minded ones. As to cultivation, where there are people who believe in it, there are people who don't; where there are people who can awake to it, there are people who can't; where there are people who are for it, there are people who are against it. Such is human society. If all people could cultivate it, awake to it and believe in it, human society would turn into a society of deities. Human society is simply the society of humankind. It won't do if it does not exist. Human society will exist forever and ever. Therefore, it is normal that some people are opposed to it. On the contrary, it would be abnormal if nobody objected to it. Without ghosts, how could humans be reincarnated into humans? Without the existence of demons, one could never cultivate Buddhahood. Without the bitter, there could never exist the sweet.

It is just because of the existence of the theory of inter-generation and inter-inhibition, people will find difficulty when they are trying to accomplish something. Only when you have succeeded in what you want to do by overcoming the difficulties through painstaking efforts, will you feel that it was not easily won, and then you will treasure what you have achieved and feel happy. Otherwise, if there were no theory of inter-generation and inter-inhibition and you could accomplish whatever you do without any difficulty, you would lead a dull life without a sense of happiness or a joy from the success.

Any kind of matter or life in the universe is composed in the same way of microscopic particles accumulating into a larger layer of particles, which are formed into surface objects as a result. Within the scope penetrated by the matter of these two different properties, all matter and all life possess dual nature in the same manner. For instance, iron and steel are very hard, but they will become oxidized and rusty when buried in the earth, while pottery and porcelain will not become oxidized when they are buried in the earth, but they are very fragile and will be broken when struck. The same is true of human beings. Humans have Buddha-nature, and they also possess demon-nature at the same time. What a human being has done without a moral code and restraint is simply dominated by his demon-nature. Whereas cultivating Buddha is removing your demon-nature and fulfilling yourself with Buddha-nature.

Human Buddha-nature is Shan, which manifests itself as compassion, altruism and the capability of enduring suffering. Human demon-nature is evil, which manifests itself as taking life, stealing and robbing, selfishness, evil thoughts, fomenting discord, stirring up trouble by rumour-mongering, jealousy, viciousness, madness, laziness, incest, and so on.

As the cosmic qualities Zhen Shan Ren differ in manifestations from dimension to dimension, the two substances of different properties in a certain dimension of the universe also differ in manifestations from dimension to dimension at the same time. The further down a level is, the more strikingly the two substances are opposed. Thus there appears a division between good and bad. The good gets better and better, while the evil gets worse and worse. The dual nature of the same object is even more complex and changeable. This is exactly what the Buddha meant by saying that all things have Buddha-nature. All things also have demon-nature, though.

However, the universe is characterized by Zhen Shan Ren. So is ordinary human society. The two substances I am talking about are simply just two kinds of matter which are countless, existing from up to down, from the microscopic to the macroscopic, and down to human society, and which can bring their duality into play when reflected in life and matter. And life and matter existing from up to down and all the ways to human society are composed of countless various matter from the microscopic to the macroscopic.

If humankind does not follow human moral standards, society will be in incurable disorder with natural calamities and human disasters. If a practitioner does not get rid of his demon-nature in cultivation, his cultivation energy will be in disorder and will not be attained, or else he follows demons in their world.

Li Hongzhi
August 26, 1996

Big Exposure

At present, a large number of practitioners have achieved the consummation, and will achieve the consummation in the future. What a solemn event it is for a human to achieve the consummation in cultivation! There is nothing in the world more splendid, more brilliant and more magnificent than this. Nevertheless, strict requirements must be made on every practitioner in the course of his cultivation, and the progress he makes at each level must reach the criterion steadily. In the perspective of the whole situation, the cultivating disciples of the Great Law are up to standard. However, there are also some ones who still cling to various attachments and fiddle about. On the surface, they also say the Great Law is good, but in reality, they do not cultivate. Especially in the general climate, all say the Great Law is good. From the upper strata of society to common people all say it is good. Some governments also say it is good. People all echo in saying it is good. Who are really sincere, then? Who are the people merely echoing what others say? Who are the people saying it is good, but in reality disrupting it? Now we have made a change of the situation in ordinary human society, where the general climate is reversed. Let's see who are still saying the Great Law is good, and who are changing their mentality. Haven't they shown themselves up in this way completely all at once?

From the incident of < *Guangming Daily*> until now, all the disciples of the Great Law have played their roles: some were firm in their genuine cultivation; some wrote straightforward to a higher authority to clarify the reputation of the Great Law; some were indignant about the irresponsible news report; however, there were also some practitioners who, in the difficult situation, did not cultivate their inner self but engaged in split activities, which made the present situation more complicated; there were also some practitioners who stopped their cultivation for fear that their standing, reputation and interests would be harmed; there were also some practitioners who spread about rumours regardless of the stability of the Great Law, which aggravated the disruption of the Law; and there were some people in charge in different areas who analyzed the situation of the Great Law with the bad habit of watching the social trends which had been developed long in political struggles. By relating the isolated problems arising in different areas together, they thought that there had occurred some social trends and passed on the information to the practitioners on purpose. In spite of various reasons for it, can there possibly be a more serious disruption of the Law than these? Worse, some stirred up trouble by rumour mongering upon their demon-nature, and desire to see chaos.

The Great Law belongs to the universe, penetrating into ordinary human society. How can it be possible that no arrangement has been made for everything and all when such a Great Law has been made public? Isn't what has happened testing Xinxing of the Dafa disciples? What is cultivation? When you say it is good, I say it is good, and everyone says it is good, how can we find out what one's Xinxing is like? It is at the critical moment that we can see what one's heart is like. Without letting go of some attachments, he even dares to betray the Buddha. Is this a small problem? Some people are afraid. But what for? My disciples! Didn't you hear me talk about a person who failed because the thought of fear came into his mind when he was on the point of attaining Arhatship? Whatever attachment of ordinary people must be given up. Some disciples said, "What to fear? My body would still be sitting there in practice even with my head off." By comparison, it is perfectly clear who cultivates well. Nevertheless, it should be regarded as a different matter that some people in charge are worried about the safety of the Great Law.

It is exactly what we try to make those disciples who did not make a further advance in cultivation see their own problems, to make those who fiddle about disclosed, to make those who disrupt the Law in disguised form exposed, and to allow genuine practitioners to achieve the consummation.

Li Hongzhi
August 28, 1996

Cultivation Is Not Politics

Some practitioners are discontented with society and politics, and cling to this intense attachment. With this, they have learned our Great Law, and then they even attempt to take advantage of our Great Law for their involvement in politics. This is an act from a dirty psychology to blaspheme the Buddha and blaspheme the Law. If they do not let go of this attachment, they will never achieve the consummation.

I emphasized again and again in my lectures that the form of ordinary human society, no matter what kind of society and politics it is, is predestined, and determined by Heaven. A practitioner does not need to bother with the affairs of the human world, still less in a political struggle. Isn't how society treats us testing a practitioner's heart? It cannot be said that we are involved in politics.

Such is the form of our cultivation of the Great Law. We won't go and seek refuge in any political forces at home or abroad, either. If those who have much control and influence are not practitioners, they can never hold any nominal or actual leading position in our Great Law.

My disciples, do remember that we are true practitioners! We have to let go of fame, interest and sentiment of ordinary people. Does what the social system is like have anything to do with your cultivation? You won't be able to achieve the consummation until you have abolished all your attachments in cultivation, without a single omission left. A practitioner won't take an interest in politics or political power other than doing his own job well, otherwise he is by no means my disciple.

We are able to make practitioners attain the Law and complete the right achievement, and also lead the people towards kindness in society, which will benefit the stability of human society. However, the Great Law is handed down not for the sake of human society, but for the purpose of your being able to achieve the consummation in cultivation.

Li Hongzhi
September 3, 1996

A Person In Charge Is
Also A Practitioner

The heads of the assistance centres in different areas can all work hard for the Great Law and are not upset by criticism. However, many of the heads cannot get along well with each other and fail to cooperate with one another in their work. As a result, this has done great damage to the image of the Great Law in people's eyes. Some people asked me if it is incapability of work. I said that was just an ordinary person's point of view. The crucial reason is that the heads and deputy heads of the centres are also practitioners who in the same way have some attachments that they cannot let go of and need an environment in which they can get rid of them. However, when a head-to-head conflict occurs, they usually push aside the conflict by using an excuse of their working for the Great Law, and saying "not cooperative", etc., instead of making use of this good opportunity to look inward for the truth so as to improve themselves. If they have not abolished their attachments and have not improved themselves, another conflict will be there for them, which will really interfere in the work for the Great Law this time. Do you know? Head-to-head conflicts in your centres are what I have arranged for you to improve yourselves. However, you used the work of the Great Law to cover up the fact that you should have improved in some aspects of your Xinxing, but you did not. When the conflict becomes serious and you cannot pass the ordeal, then you pour out your grievances to me in your mind. Do you know how I feel about it at that time? It is not that you can achieve the consummation without improving your

Xinxing simply because you work for the Great Law as a head of the centre. Even a common practitioner can realize that it is a chance for him to improve his Xinxing when he is in any conflict, why not a head of the centre? A conflict has cropped up to make you improve yourselves, and it won't do if it doesn't touch you to the very heart. Working for the Great Law is also a good opportunity for you to improve your Xinxing.

The reason why I specially write this article for you is that whatever you do and whatever you say, every act and every move you make, will have a direct influence on the practitioners. If you yourselves cultivate well, you will do well in spreading the Law in your area and the practitioners will cultivate better, otherwise you will do damage to the Law. As you are the elite of the Great Law at the level of ordinary people, I cannot merely want you to work without wanting you to achieve the consummation.

Li Hongzhi
September 3, 1996

What Is Cultivation Practice

Speaking of cultivation practice, many people would believe that by means of doing some exercises, sitting in meditation and learning some incantation, one can become a god or a Buddha or can attain the Tao. In fact, this is not cultivation practice, but merely practice of worldly skills.

In religions, great attention is paid to cultivation, which is called cultivation of conduct. In this way, it has gone to the other extreme. A monk or a nun chants scriptures diligently and regards mastery of sufficient scriptures as the way to the achievement of the consummation. In fact, in the lifetime of Sakyamuni Buddha, Jesus, including Lao Zi (Lao-tsu), there was no scriptures at all but genuine cultivation only. And the honourable masters delivered their speeches just for guiding the cultivation. The later followers committed their teachings to writing from memory and called such books scriptures. Gradually they began to study Buddhist philosophy and science of law. They did not cultivate themselves earnestly nor take the law preached by the honourable masters as a guide for genuine cultivation as in the days of the honourable masters. Instead, they took the study of religious scriptures and scholarship as cultivation practice.

This is a lesson in history. Disciples cultivating Falun Dafa, you must always remember that you can never on any account study the Law merely as scholarship of ordinary people or monks and nuns without doing genuine cultivation. Why do I ask you to study, read and learn *Zhuan Falun* by heart? It was for the purpose of guiding you in cultivation! As for those who only do the exercises but do not learn the Law, are not Dafa disciples at all. Only when you learn the Law and cultivate your mind plus the means of the consummation - practice of the exercises, and indeed to transform yourself from your nature, to further your Xinxing and to reach higher levels, can we say this is true cultivation practice.

Li Hongzhi
September 6, 1996

The Great Law Of
"A Diamond Remains Pure Forever"

Religion cannot enter into combination with politics, otherwise its leader will certainly put his heart into worldly affairs. Though he says he is trying to lead people towards goodness and encourage them to return to the pure land, he must be evil in heart and pretend to be kind, and what he really seeks must be fame and material gain. Power is what common people desire, and fame is a great obstruction to consummation. In the course of time he is bound to become the leader of an evil religion. As religion aims at teaching people to do good so that they can return to the heavenly kingdom in the end, the theory of the Law it teaches is definitely higher than the theory of human society. If it were applied to politics in the human world, it would be the most serious corruption of the heavenly Law. How is it possible that deities and Buddhas can be activated by human attachments and enter into the dirty political struggle for power in ordinary human society? This is what a man does when he is prompted by his demon-nature. Such a religion will certainly be used by a government to enter into violence and launch a religious war, thus becoming an evil religion and doing harm to humankind.

"Religion for all the people" is also not applicable. First, it is liable to change the creeds of the religion and fall into a theory for ordinary human society. Second, it is liable to turn into a political tool and corrupt the image of the Buddha Law. Third, the leader of the religion will become a politician and bring the religion into the decline of the Law, thus establishing an evil religion.

Falun Dafa is not a religion. However, future generations will take it as a religion. It is for the purpose of cultivation instead of establishing a religion that it is passed down to the people. There can be a great number of learners of the Great Law, but it won't do to turn all the people of the nation into the followers of the religion and make everybody take part in unified cultivation activities. The cultivation of the Great Law is always free. Never drag anyone in for cultivation.

Never in a period of time in the future of history can the Great Law be used by any politics. The Great Law can bring the human heart into goodness and thus stabilize society, but it is not in the least for the purpose of maintaining all these of ordinary human society that it is passed down. Disciples, do keep in mind that the Great Law can never be used by politics and power no matter how great the pressure from them will be in future.

Never have a hand in politics or interfere in national affairs. Cultivate yourselves in real earnest and move towards goodness. Keep the Great Law pure and unchangeable. Diamond is indestructible, and the Great Law will exist forever.

Li Hongzhi
September 7, 1996

Further Understanding

Of the question of Buddha-nature and demon-nature, I couldn't have given a clearer exposition. As a matter of fact, an ordeal you pass is really used for you to abolish your demon-nature. However, you have used various excuses or the name of the Great Law again and again to cover it up, you have not improved your Xinxing, and therefore have missed the chance time and again.

Do you know? As long as you are a practitioner, I will make use of any trouble and unpleasantness in any environment, under any circumstances, and of whatever you believe to be the best thing, the most sacred thing, even working for the Great Law, to remove your attachment and expose your demon-nature so that you can abolish it, because your improvement is of first importance.

When you have really improved yourselves like this, whatever you do in a pure state of mind is the best and is the most sacred.

Li Hongzhi
September 9, 1996

Admonitory Remarks

It is already four years since I began to pass down the Great Law. Some practitioners are very slow in improving their Xinxing and realm of awareness. They are still trying to understand me and the Great Law from what they feel. They always feel a deep gratitude to me for the change in their bodies and the manifestation of their supernormal capabilities. This is the understanding of ordinary people. If you do not want to change the human state of affairs and raise yourselves to a real understanding of the Great Law out of your rational knowledge, you will lose the opportunity. If you do not change the human logic of ordinary people which has stayed in your bones over thousands of years, you will not be able to shake off the shell on the surface of human beings, thus unable to achieve the consummation. You cannot always depend on me to eliminate your karma for you, while you yourselves do not really improve yourselves in the Law and jump out of human understanding and human mentality. Your way of thinking, understanding and showing gratitude towards me and the Great Law is the manifestation of ordinary people's thinking. But I am just teaching you to jump out of ordinary people and to have a real rational understanding of the Great Law.

In cultivation, you do not improve yourselves really and truly so as to bring about a great change in nature within yourselves. Instead, you rely on my power and take advantage of powerful external factors. This can never transform your human nature into Buddha-nature. If everyone of you can understand the Law from your hearts, that will be really the

manifestation of the Law whose power knows no bounds ---
the reappearance of the powerful Buddha Law in the human
world!

Li Hongzhi
September 10, 1996

The Great Law Can Never Be Usurped

My disciples! I have said again and again that the promulgation of the Great Law to human beings is already the greatest mercy to them. This has never happened for billions of years. However, there are some people who really do not know the value of it. And there are still some people who want to alter the Law or the exercises in an attempt to turn them into theirs or into something belonging to their nation and their country. Think it over! It is for the sake of the interests you are attached to or for the good of your nation and so on that you think it good. This is the understanding of ordinary people. It would be all right if you treat something of ordinary human society like this, but this is no matter of ordinary people. It is not for your nation that the Law is passed down. This is the Great Law of the universe, the essence of Buddha Law! It is to save the people that it is passed down to human beings. But have you altered such a great Law...? To alter a bit of it is to commit a monstrous sin. Be sure never to have an evil thought just because you are attached to what ordinary human society is like! It is extremely dangerous to do that!

Do you know? Some practitioners died suddenly in recent years and some of them died simply because they did such things. You should not think that your master might do something to you. You should know that there are numerous guardian gods of the Law in every dimension, whose duty is to protect the Law. What is more, the demons would not let you off likewise! It is because you cultivate the Orthodox Law that you have avoided the karma you owed in your previous existences. Once you have dropped down and become an ordinary person, there will be no one to protect you and the demons will take your life as well. And it is no use to seek protection from other Buddhas, Tao, and Gods, because they won't protect the one who disrupts the Law. Besides, your karma will also return to your body.

It is difficult for a person to cultivate himself, but is very easy for him to drop down. One is likely to change into his opposite when he is unable to go through an ordeal or cannot give up his very strong attachments of ordinary people. There are too many lessons in history. One won't feel regret until he drops down, but then it is too late.

Li Hongzhi
September 22, 1996 in Bangkok

What Is Enlightenment

Enlightenment is also called awakening of wisdom. In our Great Law, it is called opening of cultivation energy. It means that one has achieved the consummation already after completing the whole course of cultivation and is ready to enter a heavenly kingdom.

What state is an enlightened being in, then? One who has made the cultivation of Buddha is already a Buddha; one who has made the cultivation of Bodhisattva is already a Bodhisattva; one who has made the cultivation of Arhat is already an Arhat; while one who cultivates the Tao has already achieved the Tao; one who has made the cultivation of god is already a god. As some enlightened beings who have achieved the consummation need to do some things in ordinary human society or fulfill some vows, they still have to live among ordinary people for a certain period of time. But living among ordinary people like this is very hard for them. As they are far too different from ordinary people in the realm of thought, they can clearly know all the evil thoughts such as intense attachments, selfishness, filth and scheming against others, which fill the minds of ordinary people, and they can perceive the slight mental activities of thousands of people at the same time. In addition, they can also see very clearly all the karma and viruses existing everywhere in ordinary human society and many, many other bad things unknown to human beings floating and scattering in the air. The human society in the present day of the Last Havoc has tremendous karma, and people are breathing in large quantities of karma, viruses and poisonous gas. This world of ordinary people is really hard for them to stay in.

What, then, do they look like? This is also what those practitioners who have such an attachment would make a guess at. You should not watch this one like having become enlightened or that one having achieved the consummation, but put your mind into great efforts in genuine cultivation so as to achieve the consummation sooner as well. What's the necessity of watching others? In reality all those who have become enlightened are often the disciples who do not show off themselves but do genuine cultivation quietly. They are in different age groups and look no difference from ordinary people. It is most likely that they are not taken any notice of. Although they possess all divine powers and the art of transformation, they find that humans have turned out to be like low forms of life and it isn't worth making a display of their powers in front of them. Besides, seeing the display, people would also come up with various human intentions of low cognition and look at it with a human attachment of complacency, which, however, will be beyond the endurance of the enlightened beings. It is difficult for ordinary people to understand where the real great significance of the inner implication of the divine powers of Buddha Law lies.

At present, some meddlesome practitioners who do not put their minds into further advances are searching everywhere for the enlightened ones and the like. Think it over, the enlightened ones are already Buddhas and possess all that a Buddha has. How could they allow people to know them so casually? How could humans know a Buddha? When you are searching everywhere for them, your attachments, competitive mentality, show-off mentality, inquisitiveness, curiosity together with a craving mentality interfere in other practitioners' well-arranged cultivation. Do you know how they feel about this? Every act and every thought of people for a purpose will make them suffer!

As some of the practitioners have come from very high dimensions to attain the Law, they will become enlightened very soon. When I said I would give the practitioners two years for their cultivation, I was referring to these disciples. However, all the disciples of our Great Law are raising their levels very quickly indeed in genuine cultivation, and many of them will also become enlightened very soon, which is beyond the imagination of the practitioners in the past. I hope you all will set your minds to cultivation and keep making further advances unceasingly and perseveringly. I'll receive and send whoever has achieved the consummation to the heavenly kingdom.

Li Hongzhi
September 26, 1996

Remaking Of Humankind

The reality that man refers to is a foolish understanding he has of the historical development and a delusion caused by positivist science. It does not truly manifest the great reality of the Universe. Nevertheless, the authentic reality will definitely bring about new sciences, and new understandings. The Cosmic Law will make its appearance in the world once again.

Man's selfishness, rapacity, stupidity and ignorance, interwoven with his kind nature, are unknowingly accumulating all the consequences for which he will bear responsibility himself, and which are swallowing up the society. Various social problems crop up endlessly in the world beset with dangers and crises, lurking on every side. Humankind is ignorant of the fact that what has caused all these is human nature itself, and can not see that the formidable human heart is the poisonous root that results in the social problems during the moral degeneration. However, they are foolish enough to find a way out all the time in the manifestations of society. In this way, man will never realize that it is he himself who is closing himself up with all of what might be called a way out. As a result he will find no way out all the more, and the follow up will reveal even worse problems. Then, with great difficulty, he finds a bit of space, following which he takes some new measures, and closes this bit of space he has left once again. Having repeated this in the long run, he can no longer find a way out as there is no room for action, and thus the truth beyond the closed space is out of his sight. Man is beginning to suffer from all that he has reaped himself. It is in this way that the universe is to eliminate human life in the end.

The Supreme Buddha, whose compassion is immerse, has already left the Buddha Law to human beings, to whom the universe will give another opportunity. Let the great Buddha Law make the authentic reality of the universe present in the world after cleaning up all the filth and dirt as well as those stupid fallacies! Rebuild brilliance and splendour by means of the language of humankind! Cherish the value of the Buddha Law! It is just right in front of you.

Li Hongzhi
September 28, 1996

Metamorphosis

The misconduct of the clergy has totally violated the holy and pure oath they took, therefore, God's entrusting has been turned into something worthless, which shocks both humankind and the gods! Good people have always taken them as their sole dependents on whom they relied to be saved. Disappointment has caused the people more and more to lose faith in religion, in the end they have completely given up their faith in God. Thus they do everything bad and stop at nothing. Having developed up till today, people have completely become metamorphosed beings with demonic hysterics, which caused all gods to lose their confidence in humans completely. This is one of the main reasons why gods no longer take care of human beings.

Li Hongzhi
October 10, 1996

Buddha-Nature Is Free From Omission

I have mentioned many times in the Law that the appearance of the Buddhist scriptures and the Period of Decline, was caused by the fact that some people put their own words and their own understanding into the Dharma. This is the severest lesson in history. But, there are some disciples still clinging to the attachment of an ordinary person. They are dominated by their demon-nature, showing off their eloquence and literary talent, thus disrupting the Buddha Law unwittingly.

Recently some people call it "pouring out the dirty water" while practitioners talk about their cultivation experience and mention their imperfect past after they have deepened their understanding through cultivation. This completely changes the inner implications of cultivation. Cultivation is sacred. It is not something like an ordinary person's self-examination or repentance. Disciples! You cannot take a term casually and then all use it and say it. Aren't you adding something human to the Great Law? Last year the Assistance Centre of Beijing put forward the four phrases and I specially wrote an article *Correction* for it. You should have taken it seriously. Of course, there are still a jumble of other improper terms in circulation. Think of it, if one word was added today and another was added the day after tomorrow, then, with the lapse of time, the disciples of the next generation would not know whose words were and gradually the Great Law would be changed.

You must be clear that the form of cultivation I have left for you can never be altered. Don't do anything I don't do.

Don't use any term I don't use. Say what I say on cultivation. Mind! An unconscious alteration of the Buddha Law is also a disruption of the Buddha Law!

There is something more I want to tell you. Your past nature was actually built on the basis of egoism and selfishness. From now on whatever you do, you should have first consideration for others so as to attain the right enlightenment of selflessness and altruism. So from now on whatever you do and whatever you say, you must have consideration for others, for future generations, and also for leaving the Great Law intact forever.

Li Hongzhi
February 13, 1997

Sober-Mindedness

It is time for me to say something about the working methods used at present by the heads of Assistance Centres in different parts of the country. It is right to carry out the requirements of the General Society, but attention must be paid to the methodology. I often say that if what one says is entirely for the well-being of others, without the slightest purpose and understanding of one's own, the listener will be moved to tears. What I teach you is not only the Great Law, I have also left my working style to you. One's working manner of speaking and kindness plus truth can change a person's heart, but an order can never! If others are not convinced at heart and pretend to obey on the surface, they will still do their own when they are alone.

Any work of the Great Law must aim at people's attainment of the Law and the practitioners' improvement. Without these two purposes the work will be meaningless. Therefore, any activity should be organized in accordance with local conditions and the situation of the practitioners. Do avoid doing anything absolute. It is one's own free will to learn the Great Law, still less engage in activities! In fact, the heads of Assistance Centres are first of all leaders in learning the Law. If they do not learn the Law well themselves, they can not do their work well. The assemblies of exchanging cultivation experience organized by Assistance Centres in different areas should never be turned into meetings for self-criticism. Such a solemn "Law-assembly" for exchanging the Great Law cultivation experience can never be held as an exhibition to expose the dark side of the society. Above all, the practitioners can never be compelled to reveal the defects and faults they had and committed when they were ordinary people, otherwise it would cast a severely negative influence and discredit the reputation of the Great Law. You must know what you should do and what you should not do. This is nothing but solemn cultivation! The assembly for exchanging cultivation experience is intended for the improvement of the practitioners and the promotion of the Great Law, not to publicize how bad our practitioners were. It aims at cultivation of the Great Law not the so-called pour out the dirty water. Do not think the work you do for the Great Law has nothing to do with your personal cultivation. The factors improving your Xinxing are all reflected in your work. You cannot merely do your work. You should also attain consummation. I know that some few of you seldom read the Books and study the Law, and you never measure yourselves by the several scriptures as you call them that I have written for you. What is scripture? A scripture is a piece of writing that is to be read often. Do you read it? Learn the Law more and you won't get into trouble with your work. I point out your problems so that the Great Law will develop more healthily with less going wrong. In reality, the Great Law is also enriching your experience, cultivating the elite of the Great Law.

Li Hongzhi
June 13, 1997 in Hong Kong

Bear In Mind Forever

Dafa Society,

I suggest every disciple should destroy without delay all I have not made public, the materials which are in private circulation or which such as my speech spread out from Chengde, a talk about supernormal powers given by a Beijing practitioner, the speech made by the Head of Dalian Assistance Centre, the story about the Cave by the Head of Guizhou Assistance Centre and her other talks, the speeches made by people in charge in different areas, the reports given by the practitioners after they saw me, the talks given by the people in charge of the General Society of the Great Law, and the texts, the recordings and the video tapes of my speeches rearranged without permission. All these must be destroyed on the spot, and they can never be preserved on any excuse. What is the safeguarding of the Great Law? This will be a most thorough safeguarding of the Great Law, and I'll see whether you can do as I tell you to and if you are really my disciples. I tell you once more. The Law preached by Sakyamuni Buddha was damaged in this way. This is a historical lesson. From now on, nobody is allowed to tape-record or videotape talks given by any of the people in charge or any of my disciples, much less can they rearrange them into written forms or circulate them. I'm not referring to nor criticizing any particular practitioner but maintaining the Great Law. Bear in mind: with the exception of Dafa practitioners' Law-learning experience exchanges and the activities organized by the General Assistance Centres in various areas with the consent of the General society, anything that is not from the Great Law but circulating in the Great Law is disrupting the Great Law.

Li Hongzhi
June 18, 1997

A Heavy Blow

At present, in order to make cultivation convenient for more people, the practitioners of the Great Law mainly adopt the method of cultivating themselves in ordinary human society and tempering themselves at work or in other ordinary people's environment. Only those monks and nuns who have left lay life are required to wander about. However, now there are some people running about aimlessly throughout the country under the pretense of the Dafa disciples. They live in the practitioners' homes for no reason, eating, drinking, taking and asking for what they want. They go about cheating practitioners and avail themselves of a loophole in the Great Law by taking advantage of the kind nature of the practitioners. But why can't our practitioners distinguish these? Cultivation means the cultivation of oneself. Think about it. Why don't these people keep their minds on real cultivation at home? One can do his cultivation better in bad environment. Why do these people not listen to me? Why do they run about aimlessly throughout the country? Why should they ask practitioners to let go of their attachments while they eat, take and ask the practitioners for things? Have I ever taught them to do so? What is more, some people even stayed in a practitioner's home for several months. Weren't they brazenly disrupting and interfering with the practitioner's cultivation? I suggest they should pay back in full for what they ate and took by cheating, otherwise the Great Law will not forgive them. If such a case occurs again, you can report it to the police just as you treat a common cheat, because such a person can never be our practitioner.

Some so-called Law-preaching group was organized without permission, which goes about cheating practitioners in different areas. There are also some people who invite an individual practitioner to give lectures, disrupting and interfering with the practitioners' cultivation. Such people seem to be spreading the Law. They are in reality giving publicity to themselves. All the practitioners are cultivating themselves systematically according to the arrangements of my Law bodies, but only some practitioners haven't awakened to or felt it yet. Thus, aren't those people interfering? It is especially difficult for those who began to learn the Law not long ago to have a clear judgment. Some people even gave a lecture to thousands of people, talking about nothing but themselves. They went so far as to give a definition to a certain sentence of the Great Law or interpret the Great Law, with their bodies sending forth black karma and substances of attachment to the practitioners. I have made it clear in *Zhuan Falun* that nobody is allowed to do so. Why don't you think it over? Especially for those who were in charge of reception and invitation, they may have done certain intangible harm to the disciples of the Great Law, and they are not qualified to be leaders for the disciples of the Great Law. How can those people be my disciples when they don't listen to me or comply with the requirements of the Great Law? Aren't they doing something against the Great Law? Aren't they disrupting the Great Law? My disciples! You can not just realize these things until I point them out? Actually, everything is in the Law. Why don't you read the Books more? I suggest everyone of you should set your mind at rest and read my book *Essentials for Further Advances,* which you call scriptures, ten times. It is no use studying the Law when your mind is not tranquil. You should learn it with your mind tranquil.

Some few people in charge do not read the Books or study the Law, saying that the moment he reads the Law he has a headache. Isn't it quite obvious that he is being interfered with by a demon and does not want to free himself from its control? Even a new practitioner can tell the problem. How can such a person possibly remain in a responsible position of the Great Law? I think it is better for such a person to become a common practitioner of his own accord. It will do good to the Great Law and himself if he can settle down to do cultivation in real earnest for a period of time. There is also someone who had a contrary understanding of my letter of criticizing her. Not realizing what I meant by the letter, she duplicated and distributed the letter to give publicity to herself by saying, something like "The teacher wrote to me." There are some people who often use such expressions of "in the name of Master Li" when making a speech so that other practitioners will listen to and obey them. Nobody can represent me. How can your words become my words? What I say is the Law. Is what you say the Law? My disciple! I suggest you first should be a common practitioner for a period of time and pick up your job again later when you become sober-minded. No matter how much work a person in charge has done among ordinary people, he is doing voluntary service for the Great Law. His success in work is only a form of expression among ordinary people, while the people's attainment of the Law and the promulgation of the Great Law are due to the power of the Great Law itself and the specific arrangements by my Law bodies. Without my Law bodies who do these things, a person in charge would find it difficult to protect himself, let alone spread the Law. Therefore do not feel that you are someone extraordinary. There is no fame, interest or official position in the Great Law. There's nothing other than cultivation.

Li Hongzhi
June 18, 1997

Another Remark on Measuring Criterion

Recently there have been a great number of new practitioners, who need a deeper understanding of the requirements of the Great Law. Especially in some areas, some responsible people of the Great Law are also new practitioners, thus, they are required to have a deep understanding of the Great Law in a very short time so that whatever they do conforms to the Great Law. Meanwhile, the General Assistance Centres in different areas must be careful in choosing the personnel in charge. Those who lead the practitioners to act recklessly should be replaced without delay and take those who have a good grasp of the Great Law to be in charge.

Some Assistance Centres recently asked the people who supposedly had had their Celestial Eyes opened to examine the practitioners' cultivation. In fact, what those people perceived was all false images. I said a long time ago that the criterion for judging a practitioner was how good his Xinxing (mind-nature) is, and I will never allow anyone who has not attained enlightenment or consummation to perceive the true conditions of my disciples' cultivation. Those who are able to see can only see the manifestation revealed to them at a very low level, and they are unable to see things at a higher level. If a person in charge has such a person examine practitioners, the person's show-off mentality will be aroused. Moreover, his demon-nature will also interfere and make trouble, and what he can see will transform with his mind. It was wrong for the person to watch other disciples, and the one in charge who asked him to examine practitioners did not comply with my words too. Why don't you listen to your Master and judge a practitioner's cultivation by his Xinxing? Do you know? All the spaces exist in the same space at the same time. It is likely that living things in any other space will overlap with the human body. They look very much like spirit possession, but they have nothing to do with the human being as they are not in the same space. How can those who are supposed to have opened their Celestial Eyes possibly understand such complicated things?

There are still some people who will say this person or that person is possessed by spirits whenever they open their mouths. I tell you, this is simply because there is something wrong with those people themselves.

The spaces of the universe are extremely complex. What I have talked about so far is no more than what can be expressed with the human language, and there are still a lot of things that are beyond the human language. Even a disciple who has attained consummation can see nothing but what he can realize and prove when he has entered upon his achievement status, much less can a practitioner see when he is still in the course of cultivating himself.

Li Hongzhi
June 18, 1997

Foregone Conclusion

Dafa disciples, you must bear in mind that any behaviour such as dividing the Great Law into units, schools, sects or denominations by any people, at any time, in any place and on any excuse in the future will be regarded as disruption of the Law. You should never do what I do not let you do. Show-off mentality plus attachment of complacency will be most easy to be made use of by the demon-heart. What you have awakened to in the Great Law is no more than a bit of the truth which exists at a certain level, all within the boundless Law. You should never define the Law or a part of it, or even a sentence of it. If you preach your definition in public, the moment you open your mouth you have committed a sin. You would make karma that is as great as a mountain or heaven, then how can you possibly cultivate yourself? If one alters the Great Law and goes his own way, his sin will be so great that it is boundless. When paying the evil karma, he will suffer endless pain with his life being annihilated layer by layer.

The Great Law can rectify the universe, so it naturally has the powers to repress evil, put right disorder, perfect and harmonize all things, and remain invincible. In reality, many lessons have been taught in this already. Such a Law-disrupting affair will be dealt with by the guardian Gods of the Law. If you beings treasure the Great Law, you actually treasure your own life and have compassion on all beings. The Great Law is unchangeable and motionless. It lives on and on without end and always stays in the world. Thus, Heaven and

Earth will remain stable forever.

Li Hongzhi
July 1, 1997

A Dialogue With Time

Master:	Can you see what problems my disciples still have?
Deity:	Your disciples can be divided into two parts.
Master:	What are they?
Deity:	One part is those who can act according to your requirements of further advances in the Law. This part is better. The other part is those who stick to human attachment and are unable to make further advances.
Master:	Yes, I've seen it.
Deity:	You give them a process of understanding the Law, so some people came in for various purposes, but after learning the Law the majority of them were able to change their original purpose of learning the Law.
Master:	A part of them haven't changed yet.
Deity:	But for such a long time.
Master:	Yes!
Deity:	I don't think it should drag on any more if they cannot become deities. In fact, they can be only human beings.
Master:	(said to himself) They are really lost so deep in the human world. They can only be so at last, and I'm afraid they even won't be able to remain as human beings in the end!
Deity:	Actually it is not bad to be human beings in the New World. Compared with those countless high level beings who have been eliminated by

	history in the universe, they are incomparably lucky.
Master:	I still would like to wait once more, and see what they will be like when those more microscopic substances of damaging humankind have been cleaned up, and then make the decision. After all they have come to attain the Law.
Deity:	As for these people at present, some of them came to learn the Law simply because they could not find their life goal, having such a mind they don't want to change.
Master:	Most of them are among the new comers.
Deity:	Some others have one side of coming to look for the Law which they consider good for themselves, but they cannot give up the side which causes themselves to be unable to have a comprehensive understanding of the Law.
Master:	There are such types of people in the veteran disciples too, and one of the most outstanding manifestations is that: they always compare themselves with human beings, and compare themselves with their own past. But they cannot measure themselves by the requirements of the Law at different levels.
Deity:	These problems have become very serious already. It would be the best for them if they can use the way of looking into others to look into themselves.
Master:	It's time to wake them up. Their environment should be changed into a genuine cultivation

112

environment, in which they will become real deities.

Li Hongzhi
July 3, 1997

Tao-Law

For a long time all beings in the Great Law, especially the disciples, have had a misunderstanding towards the Law at different levels about the improvement of Xinxing (mind-nature). Whenever they encounter an ordeal, they fail to recognize it with their original nature. Instead, they understand it entirely with the human side of theirs. Then the evil demon will take advantage of this and give endless interference and disruption, which leaves the practitioners in the suffering for a long time. As a matter of fact, this results from a deficient understanding of the Law by the human side of theirs. Thus the divine side of theirs, or the part that has achieved success through cultivation is artificially restrained and its rectification by the Law is hindered. How can the part that has not achieved success by cultivation restrain the main consciousness and the part that has attained the Law? Because the evil demons that have been artificially fostered have availed themselves of loopholes in the Law. As a disciple, when encountering an ordeal, you will pass through it successfully as long as you remain calm and at ease or let go of your attachment to such a degree as required by different levels. If you are kept in the ordeal endlessly, you must have other problems with your Xinxing or behaviour, or the evil demon must have availed itself of loopholes in your Laissez-faire attitude. After all, a practitioner is no ordinary person. Why does the side of your original nature not rectify it?

There are two reasons for your Master to tell you this truth today: one is that your problem with this has become noticeable; the other is that you have a very deep understanding of the Law and will not understand it in a simple way.

You should also know that "naturalness" does not exist, and there is a cause for "inevitability". In fact, "natural" is a word used by ordinary people in their irresponsible arguments to justify themselves when they are unable to give an explanation to the phenomena of the universe, life and matter. They can never imagine what "nature" itself is. Under the influence of such an idea, you believe that all the ordeals are inevitable and necessary. It so happens that you have been put in a state of helplessness and a passive attitude. Therefore, you, the human side must understand it, and more important is that the side that has attained the Law should be clear about it.

Attention: It is not that I'm asking you to do something artificially, but just that I'm trying to make you understand the Law. You should have a clear understanding in this respect. In fact, the Great Law is not only intended to save human beings. It is also preached to all beings in different dimensions. One's enlightened original nature will know itself what to do. I cherish your human side so that you can go up through understanding of the Law. The Great Law is perfecting and harmonizing all beings, and all beings are also perfecting and harmonizing the Great Law. I tell you the solemnity and sacredness of the Law so as to remove your confusion and misunderstanding about the Law.

Li Hongzhi
July 5, 1997

Let Go Of The Heart Of An Ordinary Person And Persevere In Actual Cultivation

With the spreading of the Great Law, more and more people are able to recognize the Great Law. So we must pay attention to an issue: Don't bring an ordinary person's sense of hierarchy into the Great Law. All the practitioners, old and new, should be careful about this matter. Anyone who has come to learn the Law, no matter how knowledgeable he is, or how big his business is, or how high his official position is, or what special skill he has, or what supernatural powers he possesses, must practise genuine cultivation. Cultivation is extraordinary and solemn. Whether you can let go of this special heart of an ordinary person is a great ordeal which you must go through though you may find it very difficult. Anyway, as a genuine practitioner, you must let go of this attachment, because you can never achieve the consummation without abolishing it.

Veteran practitioners should also pay attention to this matter. When the number of Law learners has increased, they should attach more weight to guiding new practitioners to genuine cultivation. In the meantime, they themselves should not slack off. If circumstances permit they can spend more time learning the Law and practising the exercises. To maintain the tradition of the Great Law, to uphold the cultivation principle of the Great Law, and to persevere in genuine cultivation will be a long-term test for every Dafa disciple.

Li Hongzhi
July 31, 1997

Taking A Middle Course

In order to make Dafa disciples avoid detours in their cultivation, whenever there arises a universal or grave problem, I'll write an article to point it out promptly so that the disciples may realize it and the Great Law will suffer fewer losses. Whether to be able to take the right way depends not only on the correct cultivation of the individual disciples but also on the correctness of the form of the Great Law as a whole. So, as your Master, I often have to rectify a deviation that has arisen.

As the disciples differ in their understanding, some of them will always go from one extreme to the other. Whenever they read the Law written by me, they will behave according to it by going to extremes, which will bring about new problems. I want you to change your human way of understanding, but I don't want you to stick to the state of your human understanding of the Great Law, which, however, does not mean that you should be irrational and odd. You are required to have a sober understanding of the Great Law.

Li Hongzhi
August 3, 1997

The Law Rectifies The Human Mind

With the increase of the disciples of practising the Great Law, those who want to know the Great Law are getting more and more. However, a part of them have come not for cultivation, but for the purpose of seeking a way out in the Great Law, because they have seen there is no way out in human society. Thus it gives rise to the impurity of the practitioners' composition. At the same time, it causes the Great Law to be interfered in from another aspect as well. For example, someone derived some inspiration from the Great Law, and started something like a civilization movement in society. Such actions of usurping the Law, which originated from the Great Law but cannot verify it, will counteract the Great Law from another side as a result. In fact, any movement is unable to change the human mind in essence, its phenomena will not last long either, and people would no longer care as it gets longer. Afterwards, there will even arouse something unhealthy which is more difficult to settle. The Great Law should never come to such a state.

At present, for the good people and good deeds publicized by the media such as broadcasting, TV, newspapers, etc., many of them were done by our Dafa practitioners due to their cultivation of Falun Dafa and their improved Xinxing. However, in the reports on them, they are titled as models, backbone figures and the like, which were praised as the cause, and the deeds performed due to their cultivation of the Great Law were totally denied. This is mainly caused by the disciples themselves. Cultivation is a great and solemn matter. Why can't you tell the reporters openly and as matter of fact that you have done the deeds because you practise Falun Dafa? If the reporter doesn't want to mention the Great Law, then we simply should not whitewash any form of usurping the Law and failing to verify it. We are all becoming good people, bringing benefit to society and humankind. Why should we not have a fair and legitimate environment for ourselves? Disciples, you should remember that the Great Law is perfecting and harmonizing you while you are perfecting and harmonizing the Great Law as well.

Li Hongzhi
August 17, 1997

Principles For Disciples Of Monks And Nuns

Recently a number of disciples who are monks and nuns in the religion are cultivating the Great Law. In order to have them improve themselves as soon as possible, they should let go of the bad habits they have formed long in the religions. In this regard Dafa disciples cultivating among ordinary people should not encourage these things of theirs either. The cultivation way Sakyamuni Buddha left for monks and nuns in the temple is very good. However, the modern monks and nuns have changed it just because many of them cannot let go of their desires for money and property. For this they even invent excuses to justify what they do. For example, they explain why they build temples, set up Buddha images, print Buddhist scriptures, and say that they have to meet their expenditures in the temple, etc. All of these are not cultivation but pursuing attachments, which is entirely different from genuine cultivation. One can never achieve consummation by doing so.

Cultivating the Great Law, you should let go of your desires for money and property. If not, how can you possibly conform to the criterion of Dafa disciples? Furthermore, except in special circumstances, disciples of monks and nuns will not be allowed to take a trip by train, by air or by ship, but all on foot. Only by bearing hardships can you pay back your karma. You should beg alms with an alms bowl (you can only beg for food, never for money or things). At night you may stay at the homes of Dafa disciples in different areas, but cannot stay too long. You should be strict with yourselves! Otherwise, you are not my disciples. Because the state of cultivation for disciples of monks and nuns differs from that for disciples in worldly society, and society does not regard you as ordinary people either. In order to have disciples of monks and nuns achieve consummation as soon as possible, you should temper yourselves in the human world. You can never seek a life of pleasure, nor use any excuses to seek fame and interest. Neither can you in particular ask for money to send home. You should not have renounced the family in the first place if you can not abolish the mentality of the human world. In the old times, quite strict demands used to be set upon renouncing the family for monks and nuns. Dafa disciples of monks and nuns should be more strict with yourselves. Since you have become monks and nuns in the temple, why can you still not let go of your mentality of the human world?

Disciples! A thorough giving up of the worldly things will be done gradually for those disciples with families to abolish their attachments. However, for you disciples of monks and nuns, it is what you should first of all achieve, and it is the criterion of renouncing the family.

Li Hongzhi
October 16, 1997

Environment

The cultivation form that I have left for the Dafa disciples is the assurance for the disciples to be able to raise their levels indeed. For example, I ask you to go to the park and practise the exercises together so as to develop an environment, which is the best way to change the surface of a person. A Dafa disciple's lofty manners which have been fostered in such an environment, including whatever he says or does, can make people realize their defects and find out where they fall short, can touch others hearts, can refine people's manners, and can make people improve themselves more rapidly. Therefore, the new practitioners or self-learning disciples must come and practise at the practice sites. At present, there are about forty million practitioners in China taking part in group practice every day and there are still several millions of veteran disciples who do not often come to the practice sites (as a state of cultivation, this is normal for a veteran disciple). But as new disciples, you should never miss such an environment because all those whom you associate with in society are ordinary people, but they are the ordinary people with a rapid decline in human morality. In such a society of great dye vat you have no choice but to drift with the current.

There are still many new learners of the Great Law practising secretly at home for fear that other people will find out, which may embarrass them. Just think about it. What heart is this? General fear is an attachment that should be abolished through cultivation. How is it that you are afraid that other people will know you are learning the Great Law? Cultivation is a serious matter. How should you deal with yourself and the Law? Still others who are leaders find it embarrassing to go out for practice. If you cannot let go of such an emotion, what is there for you to cultivate? In fact, nobody is likely to know you when you go to the practice site. In some work units almost all of the several leaders are learning the Law, but they keep that secret from one another. The environment is created by you yourselves and is also a decisive factor for your improvement. I often find that you have a good mentality when you are learning the Law, practising the exercises, but when you start to work or come into contact with people, you act like ordinary people, and sometimes you behave even worse than an ordinary person. How can a Dafa disciple behave like that?

I want to take you as my disciples, but what shall I do when you yourselves do not want to be my disciples? Every attachment that you are to abolish in cultivation is a wall which stands in the way of your cultivation. You cannot do cultivation if you are still not steadfast to the Law itself. Don't regard your position among ordinary people as too important. Don't feel that you cannot be understood by others because you are learning the Great Law. Just think, the human theory that man has evolved from the ape has been given a place in the hall of great reverence, but as for such a great Law of the universe, you are ashamed even to give it a proper position. This is a real shame to man.

Li Hongzhi
October 17, 1997

Dig Out The Roots

Recently, some newspapers, radio stations, and TV stations in different parts of the country have directly mobilized those publicity machines to disrupt our Great Law, and caused extremely bad effects in the masses due to the continuous trouble-making to see the chaos in the world by some few literacy prostitutes, scientist riffraff and qigong riffraff who have invariably attempted to become famous by opposing qigong. This is a man-made disruption of the Great Law that can not be ignored. Under such extremely special circumstance, Dafa disciples in Beijing have adopted a special approach to make those people stop disrupting the Great Law. In fact, this is not wrong. It was only under the extreme circumstances that it was done (other regions should not follow their example). But the masses of student practitioners went spontaneously to these irresponsible propaganda organs which didn't know the facts to explain our actual situation, and this can not be said to be wrong, either.

What I want to tell you is not whether the incident itself is right or wrong, and I would like to point out, through such a matter, some people were exposed. They have not yet fundamentally change their ordinary people's mentality, and still used the human conception of that man defends man to understand the problems. I once said that it is not at all allowed to involve the Great Law in politics. However, the incident itself is just to call on them to learn about our true situation and recognize us in a direct and positive way without dragging us into a political end. Speaking from another angle, The Great Law enables the human heart towards good and enables the society to become stable. Nevertheless, you must be clear that the Great Law is not at all promulgated for all these, but for cultivation.

The Great Law creates the existing style at this level for the lowest mankind. Then, isn't the behaviour of various people in the existing style of the mankind at this level including collectively presenting their actual situation to whom, etc. one of the innumerous existing styles provided by the Law for the human beings at the lowest level? But only the good and the evil coexist when human beings do something. So here comes out struggle and politics. But the Dafa disciples adopted such a style, which the Law has at the lowest level in an extremely special situation, and also used all the good side. Isn't this the behaviour perfecting and harmonizing the Law at the level of mankind? It is just that such a style should never be adopted except in the extreme of devastating special circumstances.

Long ago I saw some few people not safeguarding the Great Law in their hearts, but defend something in human society. I would not be against it if you were an ordinary person, as it is a good thing of course to be a good person protecting human society. However, you are now a practitioner, and what basic point you should stand on to look at the Great Law is a matter of the root. This is precisely what I want to point out to you as well. During your cultivation, I will resort to all kinds of methods to expose all your attachments, digging them out by the roots.

You should not always depend on me to take you with me and go up while you yourselves don't move. Or you won't make a move until the Law has been made clear to you. If not made clear to you, you don't move or go in the opposite direction. I cannot admit this behaviour as cultivation. At the crucial moment, you don't follow me when I ask you to break with the human side. Opportunity knocks at the door only once. Cultivation is solemn, and the gap is becoming wider and wider. It is extremely dangerous to add anything human to cultivation. In fact, it would be all right to be able to become a good person, but you must be clear, the road is chosen by yourselves.

Through this incident, we can see several others more rushing here and there, playing a destructive role among the disciples. They didn't think deeply and correctly and put forward their own understandings to the assistance centre with good intention, but they used the worst tricks of ordinary people to spread, to sow discord and to gang up among the students. Worst still, they insanely drove the students out. Those who were driven out cultivate so many times better than you do. Have you ever thought about that? Why did you do so losing your reason and getting so angry? Could such a heart still not make you realize those strong attachments of your own? Let me tell you all, this Law is so great that it is beyond imagination, and its truth you will never know and understand all, though.

I don't pay attention to forms, but I will make use of all sorts of forms to expose your deeply concealed hearts, and to abolish them.

Li Hongzhi
July 6, 1998

For Whom Do You Exist

What is most difficult for man to let go of is his conception. Worse still, one even gave his life for a sham principle without changing his mind. However, this conception itself is to shape up after one's birth, it is not innate. Man invariably believes such ideas to be his own thoughts, which come without thinking but remain unshakable, and for which he can pay any price. Seeing the truth, he even tries to reject it. In reality, except for this pre-natal impeccable innocence, all his concepts are to shape up after his birth, not in him himself.

If the post-natal conception becomes very strong, it will simply turn its head to dominate what man really thinks and acts. At this he just thinks of it as his own thinking. Such is almost everyone of the contemporary people.

If a life can really balance the advantages and disadvantages without any concepts formed concerning a matter of great importance, then this person really can decide his own destiny. Such sober-mindedness is wisdom, but different from what ordinary people mean by intelligence. If he cannot do so, then this person is certainly dominated by this post-natal conception or outside messages. What is more, he will strive for it through his whole life, while he does not know what he has been doing during his life when he reaches old age. He has achieved nothing at all in his life but, dominated by his post-natal conception, he has done innumerous wrong things, which result in paying back his karma in his next life in accordance with the wrong things he has done himself.

When one acts impulsively, what dominates his emotional thinking is not rationality but emotion. When various concepts, such as one's belief in science, in religion, in ideology, etc., come under attack by the truth of Buddha Law, he will become impulsive in the same way. As a result, the evil side of human nature will take a leading position. Thus he is making himself even more unreasonable under the dominance of his post-natal conception, blindly following others and jumping to conclusions or complicating matters. Even those predestined will lose their good chance for this reason, making themselves deeply regret for their behaviour forever.

Li Hongzhi
July 11, 1998

Melting Into The Law

There have been more and more Dafa practitioners at present. And newcomers tend to take the lead in their perceptual knowledge, for there is no obstruction of ultra-"left" thought in society as there used to, and nor a cognitive process in ideology. As a result, it is unnecessary to take up much time in discussions learning the Law together, and plenty of time should be spent learning the Law and improving oneself as quickly as possible. The more you are filled in mind, the more rapidly you will change.

I told you in the past what a good person is and what a bad person is. It is not that a person is bad simply because he shows that he has done something bad, or a person is good because he has done something good. Someone is filled with bad thoughts in mind all over, but only does not show them yet, and the worse, remains in disguise and slick. And such a person is really bad indeed. However, someone is actually quite good, but does something wrong occasionally, and such a person is not necessarily bad. Then how could we possibly recognize a good person or a bad one anyway?

A human is just like a container. What he is filled with is exactly what he is. What he can see through his eyes and hear through his ears are all violence, pornography and intrigue against each other in literary works, and strive for personal gain, money worship, other manifestations of demonic nature, etc. in realistic society. As what he is filled with are all these things, such a person is really bad indeed no matter how he behaves. People's actions are governed by their thoughts. What sort of things can a person possibly do with a mind full of such things? It is just that people more or less have a problem of ideological contamination to a different extent, and are not aware of the problems manifested. It is because the incorrect public guidance, reflected in all different fields, is changing people without knowing it, poisoning humanity and still bringing up a large number of demonic humans with the so-called anti-traditional, anti-orthodox and anti-moral concepts. That is really the worry! Even if social economy has gone up, it will be ruined in the hands of these people because they have no human mind.

On the contrary, a person embraces good traditional ideas humanity has had for centuries, believes in being very orthodox in his behaviour and standard, and what he is filled with are all good things. What is this person's behaviour like, then? No matter whether his actions show up or not, he is really a good person.

As a Dafa practitioner, what his mind is filled with is all the Great Law, and therefore this person is definitely a genuine practitioner. So, in the matter of learning the law, you should have a sober understanding. Doing more reading and studying the Books is the key to real improvement. To make it clearer, if you read the Great Law, you are actually changing. If you read the Great Law, you are actually going up. Boundless connotations of the Great Law plus a supplementary means, practice of the exercises, will certainly enable you to reach the consummation. It is just the same to do the reading together and do the self-reading.

There is a saying from the ancients: if one hears the Tao in the morning, he may die in the evening. For today's humanity, hardly anyone can be counted as being able to really understand its meaning, do you know? If a person's mind is already filled with the Law, isn't the part that is filled with the Law assimilated into the Law? Where will that part go after the death of the hearer of the Law? I want to call on you to learn the Law more, to abolish more attachments and to let go of various human concepts, by which I mean to tell you not to take with you only a part, but the consummation.

Li Hongzhi

August 3, 1998

Catalogue Of Falun Fo Fa Scriptures :

1) **Zhuan Falun (English Version)**

2) **China Falun Gong (Revised Edition) (English Version)**

3) **Falun Buddha Law (Essential For Further Advances) (English Version)**

FALUN BUDDHA LAW
(ESSENTIAL FOR FURTHER ADVANCES)
(English Version)

Author: Mr. Li Hongzhi

Translator: Translation Group Of Falun Xiulian Dafa

Publisher: Falun Fo Fa Publishing Co.
GPO Box 3791, Central,
Hong Kong
Tel : 852-29872378
Fax : 852-29878319
Email : kwokyy@netvigator.com

Printing: Print in Hong Kong
1st Print – Dec 1998

Homepage: www.campuslife.utoronto.ca/groups/falun/

Price: **HKD25.00 (in Hong Kong)**
USD6.25 (in United States)
CAD8.80 (in Canada)
AUD10.00 (in Australia)

ISBN 962-8143-14-X